JAMAICA
Debt and Poverty

Claremont Kirton
with additional material by James Ferguson

Oxfam

© Oxfam 1992

A catalogue record is available for this book from the British Library.

ISBN 0 85598 117 2 Pb
ISBN 0 85598 116 4 Hb

Published by Oxfam
274 Banbury Road
Oxford OX2 7DZ
Designed by Oxfam Design Department   739/MJ/92
Printed by Oxfam Print Unit

Contents

Introduction

In August 1991 the United States government announced that it was to 'forgive' US$217 million of debt owed to it by the government of Jamaica. The declaration, a first step in the Bush administration's Enterprise of the Americas Initiative, followed a similar write-off the previous year of C$93 million by the Canadian government. A further series of debt-forgiveness arrangements and reschedulings are now in force or under negotiation. Britain, Germany, Japan, the Netherlands, and the so-called Paris Club of rich, industrialised nations have all agreed to postpone or cancel their claims to money owed to them by Jamaica.

Such steps are undoubtedly welcome and have been greeted with enthusiasm by the Jamaican government. Prime Minister Michael Manley described the US initiative, for instance, as 'one of great historical significance for Jamaica'. But they should also be seen within the overall context of the Jamaican debt crisis:

- According to Jamaica's Central Bank estimates, the country's debt currently stands at US$4.38 billion, amounting to approximately US$1,800 per head of the population.
- Debt servicing (the repayment of interest and principal to lender institutions) eats up 40 per cent of the foreign exchange earned by Jamaican exports.
- The 'forgiven' and rescheduled debts are mostly from low-interest and concessional loans on a bilateral government-to-government basis. Jamaica's debts are largely fixed at prevailing US interest rates and are owed to multilateral lending organisations such as the International Monetary

Fund (IMF) and the World Bank. These agencies neither forgive nor reschedule debts.

- The US government initiative actually increases Jamaica's short-term debt-servicing burden as it is conditional on the accelerated repayment of other non-forgiven debt.

- The Jamaican government currently pays out more each year to financial institutions and commercial lenders than it receives in loans and grants. In May 1991 Prime Minister Michael Manley told journalists in the US that the country would pay out US$150 million more than it would receive that year. In response, the World Bank has pledged to lend Jamaica between US$80 million and US$90 million annually between 1991 and 1995.

And so the vicious circle of borrowing and repayment continues. 'The government of Jamaica', writes Kari Polanyi Levitt, 'is in *de facto* receivership to the multilateral agencies'.[1] Unable to honour its existing debt obligations without access to more funds, it is forced to borrow more, notably from the World Bank and the IMF. In June 1991 the IMF board agreed a loan of US$59 million for the financial year 1991. Finance Minister P.J. Patterson also announced that the Jamaican government intended to approach the IMF for a three-year Extended Fund Facility rather than acting on a yearly basis.

No loan from the IMF or World Bank comes without conditions attached. The IMF lends money, principally for balance-of-payments purposes, on condition that governments implement 'stabilisation' programmes. The World Bank, for its part, insists on 'structural adjustment' policies in the economy as a whole. As the so-called lender of last resort (to which governments only turn when bankrupt), the IMF can demand policy changes in return not only for its loans, but also for recommending to other financial institutions that they should lend to the government in question.

Stabilisation and structural adjustment packages are now familiar throughout the Third World. They include the reduction of state intervention in the economy and the promotion of private-sector growth; the favouring of exports over domestic consumption as a means of earning foreign currency with which to honour debts; austerity programmes in public-sector spending and wages as mechanisms for reducing budgets and domestic demand; the privatisation of state assets and increased user-charges for social services; high interest rates in order to discourage consumption; and the devaluation of local currency in order to make exports more competitive and imports more expensive. The IMF continually monitors governments' adherence to such programmes. There are quarterly 'tests', carried out by teams of IMF consultants which governments pass or fail.

This book traces how Jamaica has followed this economic recipe. It follows the process since 1977 in which successive Jamaican governments have undergone a mounting economic crisis, growing indebtedness and an often controversial relationship with the IMF and the World Bank. It examines why Jamaica turned to the IMF, what it received, and what it has had to pay out in return. In particular, it looks at the impact of these institutions' policies on the most vulnerable sectors of Jamaican society.

The shrinking dollar

Two IMF recommendations have recently had specific repercussions for Jamaica's poor. One has been the abolition of food subsidies, traditionally a protective measure for the poor but viewed by the IMF as a 'market distortion'. In line with this thinking, the Jamaican government abolished subsidies on basic imported foods in May 1991. It also announced that the Jamaica Commodity Trading Corporation was to lose its monopoly on importing certain essential items. This state company, established in 1974, imported foodstuffs and medicines and distributed them to consumers at subsidised prices.

The IMF further recommended that the Jamaican dollar should be allowed to find its 'appropriate level'. In other words, it wanted the Jamaican government to let the currency float freely against the US dollar, leading to the devaluation which would make Jamaican exports more attractive. In September 1991 the government lifted all foreign exchange controls, thereby scrapping its special access to foreign currency through the

Central Bank and allowing the free movement of local and foreign currency. The move followed a dramatic depreciation of the Jamaican dollar over the previous year from J$8.00: US$1.00 to J$14.00: US$1.00. In the first month of free trading the Jamaican dollar fell a further 9 per cent, reaching J$18.00: US$1.00. The foreign-exchange liberalisation was intended to put an end to black-market dealing and make US dollars and other hard currency more easily available. It also contributed, however, to the rapid depreciation of the Jamaican dollar.

Because Jamaica is so dependent on importing basic goods from abroad, a drastic devaluation has an immediate and disastrous effect on ordinary consumers. Foodstuffs such as flour, rice, fish, and tinned milk are often imported and paid for with US dollars. The collapse of the Jamaican dollar, as well as the removal of subsidies, is passed on directly to the consumer who has seen food bills double within a year. At the same time, IMF-approved austerity policies are designed to hold down wages to a level under the rate of inflation. As a result, income cannot possibly keep pace with prices. For those without work the situation is even worse.

The Jamaican government has tried to offset the impact of the structural adjustment measures on the poorest by additional welfare payments and support programmes. In the 1991 budget it allocated J$407 million to schemes such as food stamps, school feeding and old-age assistance. Yet however well-intentioned and effectively targeted, these schemes cannot compensate for the drastic price increases and deteriorating services experienced by most Jamaicans.

Stories of poverty

The interviews in this book, commissioned by Oxfam in October 1991, illustrate how Jamaicans in almost every sector of society have been affected by rising prices and collapsing living standards. They also provide examples of how essential social services – health, education and housing – have been run down in the last ten years by reduced government spending. The stories they tell are of inadequate housing and dilapidated hospitals, unavailable medicines and demoralised teachers. They tell of a grim daily struggle to pay for food, clothing and transportation – even on the part of people who ten years ago would have been considered middle-class and comfortably off. The growing impoverishment of the majority of Jamaicans is revealed by several telling statistics:

- In 1989 over 30 per cent of children attending public health clinics were diagnosed as malnourished.
- In 1971 there was one doctor for every 2,700 people in Jamaica; today there is one doctor per 5,200 Jamaicans.
- In 1989 it cost on average J$1,119 to send a child to primary school, 60 per cent of this sum going towards lunch and 25 per cent towards 'fees'; at the same time, the statutory minimum weekly wage stood at less than J$100.
- According to World Bank figures, the consumption of the richest ten per cent of Jamaicans is 17 times greater than that of the poorest 10 per cent.

Whether in the squalid 'ghettoes' of western Kingston or the impoverished rural communities of St Catherine's, the toll exacted by the economic crisis is clearly visible. The crisis has many dimensions and takes different forms. In desperation, some people turn to crime. Burglaries, robberies, larceny, drug-dealing are all on the increase. In response, the police resort to brutality and frequent killings; in 1989, 180 Jamaicans were killed by the police. The fastest growing economic sectors in Jamaica are now drugs – and the security industry. Domestic violence, child abuse and drug-dependency are all serious problems.

Seeking solutions

For some Jamaicans the solution to their economic difficulties lies in escape. Throughout the late 1980s and early 1990s annual emigration figures have stood at between 30,000 and 40,000, or 80 per cent of the estimated population increase. The Jamaican diaspora, mostly now in the US but also in Canada and Britain, provides a lifeline to some families by sending back regular remittance cheques. Yet massive migration is also a sign of hopelessness, removing many qualified professionals such as doctors, nurses and teachers, from the development process.

As the formal economy collapses, the so-called informal economy grows. The number of Jamaicans involved in informal trading and services is steadily increasing. The small importers and traders, known as 'higglers', are very often employed in the formal sector at the same time. Their informal activity – importing goods from other Caribbean territories, selling clothing or electrical items on the street – allows them to supplement their inadequate formal-sector earnings.

Others have been made redundant from their formal-sector jobs and have no option but to work in the precarious world of street-vending.

There are also Jamaicans who see possible solutions not simply in individual terms, but through working with others in their communities. Both in the urban and rural areas of the island there are groups which attempt to escape from poverty by starting small-scale enterprises and associations. These community-based initiatives may be agricultural – producing food for local consumption – or they may be involved in producing other goods and services. In many cases they are encouraged and supported by local NGOs and by agencies such as Oxfam. The Oxfam programme in Jamaica emphasises the importance of community self-organisation, not only as a basis for economic activity but also as a means to obtain access to better services.

There is much debate among Jamaicans, whether involved in such organisations or not, about the debt crisis and its possible solutions. High on the list of priorities is the idea of increased self-reliance, of reducing Jamaica's costly and illogical dependence on imported foodstuffs and essential goods. This would imply a conscious policy shift towards domestic production and import-substitution. There is also the widespread belief that the Jamaican government should reduce, or stop altogether, its borrowing from the IMF and World Bank. This reflects the attitude of many that the poor received little benefit from the borrowing of the 1980s yet are being asked to bear the brunt of the resulting structural adjustment policies. Few people would advocate a unilateral cessation of debt-servicing, however; popular ideas are that Jamaica should pay only a fixed percentage of its export earnings in debt repayments, or that repayments should be postponed or reduced by agreement with the IMF and World Bank to manageable proportions.

In the current climate of 'forgiveness' it remains to be seen whether the international financial institutions would contemplate such a serious reduction in Jamaica's crippling burden of debt. Until they do, Levitt's image of Jamaica as a drowning man will remain sadly appropriate:

> Jamaica is in the position of a drowning man, treading water to keep afloat, but slowly drifting further offshore. Cries for help in the form of annual begging missions to bilateral donors, and acceptance of new loans from official agencies carrying conditions of the kind already described, have produced just enough assistance to keep the country afloat, and able to service debt, for a few more months, hopefully even years. Reschedulings, debt write-off, and grants by the bilaterals, whose loans are, on the whole, softer than those of the Fund and the Bank, are enabling Jamaica to continue to service mulilateral debt which, as is well known, cannot be rescheduled or refinanced.[2]

Spreading fertiliser in a sugar plantation. Workers are not given adequate
protection, and suffer skin and other health problems.

2

An overview of the economy of Jamaica

2.1 Historical background

A sizeable percentage of the population of Jamaica could be described as 'poor and powerless'.[1] Poverty can be understood as a state of relative deprivation; people are 'poor' when they cannot obtain the resources to acquire the type of food and other necessities of life, and cannot maintain the living conditions, which are customary in their societies. The poverty of the Jamaican people has shown itself through high levels of material deprivation; and the majority of poor people have remained 'powerless' in the sense that they are unable to exercise any control over either the established institutions of authority in their society, or the means of production.

Jamaica's historical experience was no different from that of the wider English-speaking Caribbean. European invasion, near the end of the fifteenth century, was based on plunder and trade. The indigenous Arawak-Carib Indians were decimated and their primitive communal societies totally destroyed. Then followed the introduction of slavery and the slave trade.

The slave trade lasted for nearly four centuries, and according to Eric Williams:

> ...kept the wheels of metropolitan industry turning; ...it gave sustenance to new industries based on the processing of colonial materials; it yielded large profits which were ploughed back into metropolitan industry; ...and made the Caribbean territories among the most valuable colonies the world has ever known.[2]

Some fifteen million people were transported through the 'Middle Passage' from Africa to the Caribbean and North America. For those who survived the terrible voyage, conditions on the slave plantations were horrendous; characterised by extreme physical brutality, extreme poverty, malnutrition, and low life-expectancies. While the slave trade flourished, it was 'cheaper' to replace dead slaves with newly-shipped ones rather than provide adequate working conditions.

Sugar-cane cultivation on plantations, using initially African slave labour and then indentured migrant labour mainly from India, dominated this period of Caribbean history. The economies of the islands were oriented towards meeting the raw material requirements of European industry, and any potential for Caribbean economic development was stifled because the surpluses available for investment were all transferred abroad. One of the major features of contemporary Jamaican economy emerged at that time; specialisation in the production and export of primary products, and importation of almost all of the products required locally for both production and consumption.

During the struggle against slavery in Jamaica, independent 'Maroon settlements' of ex-slaves were established. The Maroons had fought for most of the seventeenth and eighteenth centuries against the British, using a form of guerrilla warfare which baffled most of the forces sent to subdue them. In 1739, Cudjoe, the Maroon leader, and Colonel Guthrie, representing the British, signed a peace treaty under the terms of which the Maroons were guaranteed freedom and allocated land, in exchange for a cessation of all hostilities.

When Emancipation came in 1838, the ex-slaves had no land, finance or even basic tools to start a new independent life. Many were forced either to work for subsistence wages on the plantations or farm 'captured'(or 'squatted'), often poor quality, lands. The emerging Jamaican peasantry continued to face difficulties in obtaining land. It was only after the British Government realised that social stability could only be maintained by making more land available to small-scale farmers, that attempts were made to introduce land settlement schemes in the late nineteenth century.

The Churches in Jamaica played a role in the development of

education following the abolition of slavery. With financial assistance from people in England and from a few Jamaicans, attempts were made to establish church schools. But funds were limited, and as a result the few schools which were set up, and the education they were able to offer, were of a low standard.

World-wide economic depression in the 1930s affected the countries of the Caribbean, and caused instability throughout the region. In Jamaica, the social unrest culminated in the 1938 revolts. Following these disturbances, the British Government responded by appointing a Royal Commission of Inquiry (the Moyne Commission).[3] In its Report, this Commission recommended the improvement of social services, increased financial aid to the region from Britain, the provision of some guarantees for regional agricultural exports to the United Kingdom, and the implementation of land settlement schemes to reduce the conflicts between the small farmers and the large landowners over access to land and other resources. These recommendations led to the establishment of the Colonial Development and Welfare Committee, which was intended to provide policy direction to the Caribbean colonies.

Heavy dependence on primary products makes the Jamaican economy vulnerable to fluctuations in the global market. These sugar-refinery workers have little job-security.

BELINDA COOTE/OXFAM

By the time it gained political independence in 1962, Jamaica was still underdeveloped, dependent, and poverty-stricken. The new government's economic policy and programmes were significantly influenced by the contemporary Puerto Rican experience of 'Operation Bootstrap'. This was an economic development programme which was heavily dependent on foreign capital being attracted to invest in the country by the provision of generous government incentives.

Jamaica's own version of this policy led to increased penetration by multinational corporations from the United States and Canada in the major productive sectors, including bauxite and tourism, and also in the financial sector. The country became increasingly dominated by foreign capital,[4] which led to increases in the transfers of surpluses abroad and did little to improve the situation of ordinary working people.

2.2 The structure of the Jamaican economy

Jamaica can be simply described as a small, open, dependent, capitalist economy. It is 'small' both in terms of population (2.4 million people) and geographical area (10,992 square kilometres); the small size of the population and the relatively small per capita Gross Domestic Product (GDP), which was only US$1401 in 1990, limits the size of the national market and this has implications for domestic production.

The Jamaican economy is 'open' in the sense that foreign trade, as evidenced by high levels of exports and imports, accounts for a significant proportion of GDP. The Jamaican economy is also 'dependent' in that it relies heavily on the developed economies of the US, Western Europe (mainly the UK), Canada and Japan for trade, economic and financial assistance, technology and management, and for preferential market access in respect of two of the major commodity exports, sugar and bananas.

It is a predominantly 'capitalist' economy: production, distribution, and exchange are organised so that maximising private profit is the single most important objective. Not unexpectedly, there is an inherent bias in the economy against small-scale firms, which face considerable difficulties in obtaining finance, acquiring modern technology, and finding markets. These small businesses face considerable competition from larger firms, and many of them fail, with the owners losing whatever amounts of capital they may have invested.

The country's economic structure has historically showed certain features, which can be traced from their origins in the early colonial years. There has been over-specialised production of a narrow range of primary products, mainly for export, with sales limited to a few markets. The country's export industries are directly linked with the advanced capitalist countries through the use of imported management, technology and raw materials, and dependent on foreign finance and foreign markets. The links between the export industries and the rest of the national economy have been limited.

The prices for these export products have been unstable and this has led to wide fluctuations in domestic levels of income and employment, and to chronic economic problems.

The country has been characterised by a heavy dependence on imports and on foreign capital inflows. Imports of consumer goods continue to account for over 20 per cent (1989 figures) of total imports; food imports average around ten per cent of total imports. Raw materials accounted for an annual average of nearly half of total imports over the last five years. On average, foreign capital inflows have accounted for about one-quarter of total foreign exchange receipts in recent years.

Jamaica has suffered from a lack of economic autonomy; there has been a predominance of foreign decision making in the country's economic activity partly as a result of the historical experience of foreign ownership and control over important sectors of the economy, and partly because of the country's dependence on financial assistance from individual countries and multilateral organisations such as the IMF and World Bank. Bilateral assistance has in the past usually involved conditional agreements on the widespread use of donor country personnel, materials and equipment.

The locally-generated surpluses from economic activities have been transferred abroad by various methods, including normal profits transfers and irregular methods such as invoice manipulation. As a result, very little capital has been available for reinvestment locally.

Over the years, many people in Jamaica have lived in poverty, with inadequate housing, inadequate food, and limited provision of social services such as health and education.[5]

There are, however, some sections of the national economy which have attempted to struggle against dependence on foreign capital and foreign markets. These include small businesses and micro-enterprises (recently estimated at over 30,000), some large domestic manufacturers, and thousands of small farmers. What these types of economic enterprises have in common is their use of locally-produced raw materials in their production processes, and the fact that they produce goods mainly for local consumption. Over the years, these economic activities have received support from the more nationalist political leaders.

There also exists a large informal economy engaged in both legal and illegal economic activities, in which a significant proportion of the country's population are active participants. Its roots exist in the period of slavery, but its size and scope have increased significantly over the last decade or so.[6]

Performance 1950-70

The Jamaican economy showed an impressive rate of economic growth during the post-war years up to 1970. GDP grew at an annual average rate of nearly seven per cent during the 1950s and 60s.[7] The fastest rate of growth of the Jamaican economy during this period occurred between 1950 and 1955, when real GDP increased at the rate of 10.1 per cent per annum. The reason for this particularly spectacular rate of growth is that at this time, significant economic expansion was occurring in the bauxite-alumina industry and the domestic construction sector.

During the period 1950-70 certain changes took place in the country's economic structure, particularly in the relative importance of the mining and the agricultural sectors. In 1950, the bauxite sector made a negligible contribution to GDP, but by 1970, this sector had increased its contribution to 12.6 per cent of total GDP. Other sectors of the economy which showed significant growth over the period were construction, manufacturing and distribution. However, at the same time, the contribution of the agricultural sector to total GDP declined from nearly one-third to less than one-tenth.

2.3 Economic crisis in Jamaica: explanations and effects

Crisis : some views

Over the years, Jamaica, like most developing countries, has experienced various economic crises, of different degrees of intensity. These crises have, since 1970, led to serious economic and social dislocations in the country, including a general deterioration in living standards for the majority of Jamaicans, increased unemployment, greater inequalities in the distribution of income and wealth, a reduction in social services, high rates of migration of skilled people, significant growth of the informal or underground economy, massive flight of capital and increased criminal activity and drug abuse.

There are many different theories which have been put forward to explain economic crises in countries like Jamaica.[8] These include suggestions that the crisis is characteristic of all post-colonial states and results from severe weaknesses in their institutional, ideological and leadership structures. Others contend that the crisis results from the global geopolitical struggles of socialism and capitalism or super-power rivalry. Another view is that such a crisis is locally based and has arisen because of persistent dislocation in the economy.

Crisis in Jamaica

In the case of Jamaica, the crisis can only be explained in terms of changes which have occurred both in the world economy and within the Jamaican economy itself. The crisis has its roots in both external circumstances, as well as internal factors particular to Jamaica.

Up to the 1970s, Jamaica benefited from the boom conditions in the world economy. In the postwar period up to the early 1970s, policies geared towards attracting foreign investment as part of the 'industrialisation by invitation' strategy were implemented.There were large inflows of foreign capital for investment in the bauxite/alumina sectors, manufacturing and the tourism industries. With these foreign capital inflows, by 1970, the Jamaican bauxite industry became the largest in the world producing 12 million tonnes of bauxite per year, which was 21 per cent of total world output. There were some positive though limited spinoffs for the rest of the economy as a result of these foreign capital inflows; however, the bulk of the profits generated by these activities were transferred abroad by the controlling companies.

1972-76

However, in spite of the boom conditions existing in Jamaica during the first decade of Jamaica's political independence (1962-72), at the time of the People's National Party's (PNP) election to government in 1972 there were widespread social problems. Unemployment was very high, at 23.2 per cent in 1972, and there was massive migration of both skilled and unskilled Jamaicans. Limited educational provision had resulted in a high level of illiteracy, and a large percentage of ordinary Jamaicans were poorly housed and inadequately fed.

The PNP government introduced a range of measures to attempt to tackle these problems. Government expenditure on social services increased, with especial emphasis on health-care and education. In 1976, minimum wage legislation was introduced, to protect the poorer sections of the working population. The government also carried out selective take-overs of various foreign enterprises, including public utilities, sections of the sugar industry, the flour-refining plant, and a few financial institutions and hotels; and a tax was imposed on the operations of the foreign bauxite-alumina companies.

The Jamaican economy was affected by a number of adverse developments in the world economy during the early 1970s, of which the most important was the 1973 oil price increase. Jamaica's oil import bill trebled between 1973 and 1974. In addition, the country's terms of trade - the difference between the prices received for exports and the cost of imports - worsened during this period. Payments for imports rose while export earnings fell.

These developments led to a serious deterioration in Jamaica's balance of payments, with the deficit on the current account of the balance of payments rising to nearly US$300 million in 1975. Also[8], the inflow of private capital to finance direct foreign investments - which had provided some support for the balance of payments during the 1960s - began to decline in the early 1970s.

1976-80

The four years between 1976 and 1980 were probably the most traumatic in the post war economic history of Jamaica. The economy was in steep decline and unemployment rose rapidly, as did prices in the shops. The level of foreign debt rose as the government was forced to borrow to cover its balance of payments difficulties. The quality of life declined for most people, and these years were marked by an unprecedented level of violence of both a political and criminal nature.

The serious balance of payments problems which had emerged earlier in the decade forced the Government to seek external financing from the International Monetary Fund (IMF). Two agreements with the IMF were signed – in 1977 and 1978 – but financial support from the IMF was suspended in both cases because the economy had failed to meet the performance targets upon which IMF support is conditional. During the second half of the 1970s there was also a marked reduction in the availability of external funds from commercial banks. As a result the government's fiscal deficit – the difference between government revenues and expenditures – had to be financed in part by Central Bank credit creation (in effect, the printing of money); but this exacerbated both inflation and the balance of payments deficit.

The 1980s

The economic crisis was a major reason for the defeat of the PNP in the 1980 general election and its replacement by the Jamaica Labour Party (JLP), a party then oriented much more towards free-market economic policies than its predecessor. Because the JLP's economic philosophy was more in tune with thinking in the multilateral lending institutions and in the US, it was expected that the government would be able to mobilise a large increase in external financial support, especially from concessional sources, and that this would help to revitalise the economy.

There was a modest recovery in economic growth in the early 1980s but adverse developments in the wider world economic climate again had serious consequences for Jamaica. The world recession in 1981/1982 reduced the demand for the country's exports of primary products, and in particular bauxite/alumina, and this led to a worsening of the balance of payments position. As a result a number of major economic measures were undertaken, supported by the IMF, in an effort to restore some viability to the country's economy and to reduce the balance of payments deficit. They included devaluation of the currency, an increase in taxation, cuts in government expenditures, the removal of import restrictions and the abandonment of price controls. Whatever effect they may have had on economic indicators, these stringent and wide-reaching measures had a serious impact on living standards throughout the country.

Despite the best efforts of the government to carry out the recommendations of the international lending institutions, the economy was on several occasions unable to meet the stringent performance criteria demanded by the IMF, with the result that agreements for external financial assistance were again temporarily suspended.

Although falling oil prices provided some respite in 1986, the economy was unable to overcome its severe structural macroeconomic imbalances: the inability to earn sufficient foreign exchange to pay for the country's import and debt servicing needs, and the inability of the Government to generate sufficient revenue to cover its necessary expenditures. By 1989, the PNP, which had regained power from the JLP in February of that year, found it necessary to implement a wide-ranging stabilisation programme which included further cutbacks in government recurrent and investment expenditures, increased taxes, higher prices for basic goods, restrictive credit policies and the sale of public property, especially hotels. There was also further devaluation of the Jamaican dollar.

The programme was extended in January 1990 with the backing of the IMF, which provided almost US$100 million in loan finance to the Government. Additional measures were implemented including higher interest rates, and an increase in the prices of petrol and electricity. The aim of this programme, as with previous IMF-backed stabilisation packages, was primarily to reduce domestic demand from both the public and private sectors and therefore to bring about a cutback in spending on goods and services. The intention was to ease the pressure on the balance of payments.

Trends in Jamaica's external debt

Most of the debt was contracted between 1975 and 1985 in order to finance the Government's fiscal deficit and to provide short-term support for the balance of payments. Most of the debt is owed to official creditors – multilateral lending agencies such as the IMF and World Bank and bilateral donors such as the US.

The need to service the country's external debt by repaying principal and interest has created serious problems for both the finances of the Government and the economy in general. Actual debt-servicing payments accounted for 47 per cent of foreign exchange earnings from exports in 1987; the burden has been reduced somewhat since then, with 26 cents out of every dollar of foreign exchange earned now being used to service Jamaica's debt, according to 1991 government figures. Some economists, however, dispute this figure.

2.4 Responses to economic crisis: stabilisation and adjustment

In general, developing countries have responded to economic crises by adopting various combinations of the following policies:

- Borrowing from abroad to finance the balance of payments deficits.
- Restricting international trade and payments links with the rest of the world.
- Adjusting the domestic economy to correct internal and external economic imbalances.

However, there are problems with all of these strategies. Access to funds from abroad to finance balance of payments deficits has become much more restricted during the 1980s and early 1990s. Attempts to restrict international trade and payments relations can generate serious domestic economic and social dislocation especially in heavily import-dependent economies. In addition, policies which attempt to restrict capital outflows also can generate further domestic economic chaos by creating conditions for the emergence and growth of foreign currency black markets and capital flight.

In attempting to adjust their economies so as to reduce internal and external imbalances, many, though not all, developing countries have tended to use IMF/World Bank policy approaches. Jamaica has relied heavily on IMF/World Bank support. The IMF programmes focus on economic stabilisation, while those of the World Bank emphasise structural adjustment.

As we have seen, the IMF/World Bank strategies implemented in Jamaica have led, amongst other things, to currency devaluation, which was expected to reduce the country's import bill and promote its exports; reduced government expenditure, especially on social infrastructure and social services; and the removal of various government subsidies. In addition, governments at various times have introduced revenue-generating measures such as increased taxation and the sale of government property and other enterprises to the private sector. Finally, the implementation of wage guidelines which restrict wage increases, and increases in domestic rates of interest have been introduced in an attempt to reduce demand.

2.5 Effects of structural adjustment

Balance of Payments

One of the major objectives of the stabilisation and structural adjustment programmes undertaken by Jamaica over the last 15 years relates to improvements in the country's balance of payments position. During this period, however, the country experienced a negative current account balance every year since 1975. An examination of the trade balance data shows that only in 1977 and 1978 did export earnings exceed import payments. During the same period, the official exchange rate moved from J$ 0.91: US$1.00 in 1975 to J$8.00: US$1.00 in 1990, reflecting the devaluation-led policies of the IMF. In the course of 1991 and 1992, the Jamaican dollar underwent a further dramatic series of devaluations, falling to J$22.7: US$1.00 by February 1992. This was a consequence of the government's exchange-rate liberalisation policy.

Up-market shopping centre, Kingston. Successive devaluations have resulted in higher prices for consumer goods and a real loss of purchasing power for wage earners.

It is clear, then, that the massive devaluations carried out under the direction of the IMF have failed to generate the anticipated positive balance of payments responses. On the contrary, because the Jamaican economy is so heavily dependent on imports of basic foodstuff, oil and related by-products, as well as essential productive inputs for the critical economic sectors, including agriculture and manufacturing, such devaluations have had the effect of increasing import prices and have thus generated high rates of domestic price increases. In turn, this has led inevitably to increases in the price of domestically produced goods and services, and a declining level of real purchasing power on the part of wage and salary earners, and increases in profits of many entrepreneurs who could easily pass on higher prices to consumers. During this same period, government foreign borrowing to finance balance of payments deficits showed a significant increase. Total government debt in nominal terms moved from US$688 million in 1975 to US$4032 million in 1989. In early 1992, despite much-publicised 'forgiveness' and rescheduling, the debt remained at more than US$4000 million.

Estimates of capital flight from Jamaica[9] indicate that between 1976 and 1980 nearly US$500 million left the country, while between 1981 and 1984 approximately US$240 million were transferred abroad outside of the official channels. At the same time, it has been estimated that the foreign currency black market rates increased significantly, with the differential between the black market and official rates reaching a high of 120 per cent in 1977. The average of differentials for the period 1977 to 1980 was 46 per cent and that for the period 1981 to 1985 was 32 per cent.

Economic growth indicators

Between 1975 and 1980, Jamaica experienced a falling-off in real economic growth every year. All the major economic sectors, especially the mining and construction sectors, experienced massive negative growth rates in 1975 and 1980. Since 1980 there has been some improvement in the economic growth indicators as evidenced by positive GDP growth rates from 1981 to 1983 and improvements in real wages. However, in 1984 and 1985 Jamaica's real GNP fell by 2.5 per cent and 5.9 per cent respectively. During the same period, real wages fell by 17 per cent. In May 1991, Prime Minister Michael Manley announced that the national minimum wage would be raised from US$14 to US$17 per week. According to the Economist Intelligence Unit, 'Jamaica currently ranks as one of the cheapest labour markets in the region'.

Estimates indicate that since 1975 the size of the informal economy has increased. It seems to be the case that, faced with the negative consequences of economic stabilisation and adjustment programmes, Jamaican households and business enterprises have responded by increasing their levels of involvement in informal economic activity.

The social impact of stabilisation and adjustment

There are three main indicators which can be used to assess the effects of stabilisation and structural adjustment on household living standards. Firstly, income levels and income distribution, which will be affected by changes in employment and wage levels. Secondly, the prices of critically important commodities and services, especially food and selected non-food items, such as housing and transportation, which will be affected by, for example, devaluation, the removal of subsidies, or changes in government policy on regulation of imports. Thirdly, the levels and composition of government expenditure, which will have implications for social services, especially health and education.

It must be remembered, however, that since households in Jamaica are far from being homogenous, the damaging effects of the stabilisation and adjustment programmes will not be uniform across the whole of society. Those most likely to be hardest hit are the poorest segments of society, people who tend to have neither access to political representation and related patronage, nor 'contacts' in the government sector. Poorer people also have no access to savings which they could use to cushion the effects of falling incomes. In addition to the heavy impact on low-income households in general, there are other especially vulnerable or disadvantaged groups such as children, elderly persons and the disabled, all of whom are likely also to bear the brunt of such programmes.

In implementing adjustment measures, many developing countries have failed to give serious attention to the damaging effects on poor people in their societies. The result, therefore, has tended to be increasing levels of poverty, as more and more people become unable to attain minimal living standards.

Poverty, income and welfare distribution

Jamaica has historically been characterised by severely inequitable income distribution to the extent that the country could almost be said to consist of 'two Jamaicas'. A recent Survey of Living Conditions (SLC)10 conducted by two government agencies found that the average consumption of the top ten per cent of Jamaicans is sixteen times as great as that of the bottom ten per cent.

Recent estimates show that one out of every three Jamaicans have household expenditures which put them below the national poverty line. The majority of those living below the poverty line (70 per cent) are to be found in the rural areas of Jamaica, where just over half of the country's population live. At the same time, of the wealthiest 20 per cent of Jamaicans, two out of every five

JANET MCCRAE/OXFAM

Only a third of Jamaican households have an inside piped water supply.

live in the capital and its environs.

An evaluation of housing quality of the different economic strata in Jamaica is quite revealing. The Survey mentioned above examines the materials from which houses are constructed, sources of drinking water, and availability of electricity. Nearly half the dwellings of the poorest 20 per cent of Jamaicans are built of wood, which is potentially dangerous, especially in hurricane-prone areas. By comparison, seven out of every ten homes belonging to the top twenty per cent of the population are constructed out of concrete blocks reinforced with steel.

In examining access to drinking water, the Survey found that about one-third of Jamaican households get their drinking water from a piped indoor supply, with some 40 per cent using outside taps, and the remainder using rainwater and natural sources. Piped water is assumed to be relatively 'safe' when compared with water from natural sources. Among the poorest 20 per cent, less than one in every ten homes have piped water indoors, while over six out of every ten homes in the wealthiest 20 per cent have indoor taps. It is interesting to note that over one-third of the poorest households get their water for domestic use either from rainwater or natural sources such as rivers and springs. With 'safe' water less accessible to the poorer groups one can reasonably infer that their health will be badly affected, especially since 'unsafe' drinking water is one of the major causes of infant diseases in developing countries.

With regard to electricity supply, the available data shows that for the poorest 20 per cent of Jamaican homes, only three out of every ten have electricity while for the wealthiest 20 per cent the figure is nine out of ten. In the capital, about one-fifth of homes, mainly in ghetto areas, do not have electricity.

Unemployment

Adjustment measures are likely to generate increases in unemployment for a number of reasons. Firstly, with contractions in government expenditure, public sector workers are likely to become unemployed. Secondly, total demand is likely to be reduced thus forcing private firms to cut back on output and also reduce employment. Thirdly, with increasing interest rates as part of monetary policy, the cost of borrowing increases and businesses respond by reducing production levels.

In examining welfare, it is useful to look at unemployment trends. Over the last 15 years unemployment has averaged 24 per cent per annum, peaking at 31.1 per cent of the labour force in 1979. The data show that female unemployment rates are generally more than twice those for male unemployment. With about four out of every ten Jamaican households headed by women, higher female unemployment rates imply poorer living conditions for these particular families.

When we examine unemployment rates by selected age groups, we find unemployment rates among women in the 14-19 age group averaging over 80 per cent in 1979-1982, but declining to 60 per cent in 1989. For the age groups 20-24, six out of every ten female members of the labour force were unemployed in 1982, but this had declined to four out of every ten in 1989. Women in the 25 to 35 years age group were slightly better off, with four out of every ten being unemployed in 1982, declining to two out of every ten in 1989. Male unemployment rates are significantly lower in all age groups than in the corresponding female age groups. With unemployment rates for women much higher than men, the difficulties facing those forty per cent of

Jamaican households which are headed by women are tremendous.

In the absence of any unemployment benefits, those facing abject poverty can access the government's Poor Relief Programme. This Programme is established to provide the 'destitute' with care and assistance in selected institutions and under non-institutional arrangements. Institutional care is provided in infirmaries. Non-institutional support takes the form of financial and food assistance. In June 1991, the government estimated that 70,000 Jamaicans were receiving J$50 (US$5) monthly in food stamps. A weekly payment of J$30 (US$3) was also made to 56,000 claimants from the National Insurance Scheme.

Changes in prices of food and non-food items

Stabilisation and adjustment programmes almost inevitably lead to increases in the general level of domestic prices for food and other basic necessities. This is usually as a result of currency devaluation which leads to increases in import prices, generating increases in all other domestic prices. Where a country imports a significant amount of its food requirements, devaluation can lead to a spiralling of food prices. The removal of food subsidies as a way of reducing government expenditure also places upward pressure on food prices.

Wage rates frequently fail to keep pace with rising consumer prices because when the economy is in recession, there is a reduced demand for labour. In addition, government action to reduce expenditure and introduce wage restraints, such as imposing a wage 'freeze' or a severe limit on wage increases, is very often part of the adjustment package.

When wages and salaries are frozen, then the real incomes of many people will fall and their ability to purchase commodities will decline. This is a conscious policy goal since it is argued that reduced expenditure will automatically mean reduced imports, and with falling imports the balance of payments position is likely to improve. Of course, it is clear that the basic nutritional intake of a large percentage of the population will actually decline as a result of reduced purchasing power.

The All Items Consumer Price Index (CPI) shows changes in

prices. For Jamaica, prices increased by an annual average of 17 per cent between 1975 and 1989. Between 1976 and 1980, the annual average inflation rate was over 20 per cent. During 1984 and 1985, however, in the wake of IMF adjustment measures, prices increased by over 25 per cent annually.

The price of food has increased at rates which are even faster than other items consumed locally; to the extent that 'food and drink' are estimated to account for over half of the expenditure of Jamaican households, these price increases have seriously affected the living standards of the poorer people. A recent study claims that food prices in Jamaica are only slightly lower than those in the United States, where the minimum wage is 11.5 times as high. In November 1989, for instance, a pound of chicken in Jamaican markets cost the equivalent of US$106.

The cost of feeding a family of five in Jamaica has risen astronomically since 1979, from J$24.27 to over J$220 as at June 1990. Data provided by the Nutrition Department of the Ministry of Health shows the stark deterioration in the situation facing Jamaican poor people who earn the minimum wage. In June 1979, one minimum wage of J$26.00 earned by a household could meet the cost of feeding a family of five for a week. However, during the 1980s under the IMF/World Bank adjustment programme, a similar food basket purchase required between two and three times the minimum wage. Recently the minimum wage has been increased to J$120 per week, but with rising food prices this can barely purchase half of what is required to feed a family of five for a week.

With increasing food prices, the nutritional status of poor people has worsened. Although it is possible that some families may be able to offset the rising food prices by income-generating informal economic activities, there has been an increase in poverty-related illnesses particularly among young children. The number of children admitted to the main children's hospital in Kingston suffering from malnutrition and malnutrition-gastroenteritis has more than trebled since 1978. Over three out of every ten children attending public health clinics in 1989 were diagnosed as being malnourished.

Successive governments have attempted to cushion the negative effects of IMF/World Bank measures on food consumption levels of poor people. In 1984, the JLP introduced a Food Stamp Programme to assist groups considered to be nutritionally 'at risk'. This programme provided bi-monthly amounts of J\$20 in food stamps (currently J\$50 per month) so that recipients could obtain basic foods such as cornmeal, rice and skimmed milk at various shops. There were two categories of recipients; firstly, there were pregnant and lactating women, and young children, with neither group being subject to any means tests. Secondly, there were poor and elderly persons, who were provided with assistance only after an assessment of their financial needs.

The programme suffered from a number of weaknesses. The levels of government funding provided satisfied the needs of only one-quarter of those registered persons eligible to receive food stamps. Some people used the stamps for purposes other than the purchase of the specified food commodities. The programme could be, and was, used as an instrument of political patronage; some high-income households received the benefits. Consequently, particularly in view of the declining purchasing power of the food stamps in the context of rising food prices, the present Manley Government has reduced the number of eligible persons and has also decided, as part of structural adjustment measures, to eliminate the last food subsidies in the course of 1992.

Housing

Housing problems have plagued the country over the last two decades, with excess demand for housing leading to phenomenal increases in both house prices and rentals. Between 1987 and 1989, an average of 2,716 houses were completed yearly, with the public sector accounting for 90 per cent of these. This building programme has satisfied only about 15 per cent of the total demand for houses.

Housing costs have increased significantly, largely as a result of increasing import prices following the numerous devaluations of the Jamaican dollar. The housing sector is characterised by a high import content, particularly of construction materials. The price of locally produced materials also increased during the period. In 1989, for example, the price of lumber rose by 20 per

House prices in middle-class areas such as this have risen enormously as a result of structural adjustment measures.

cent, steel by over 25 per cent, cement by 28 per cent, and paint by 25 per cent.

Housing costs have also risen as a result of increasing interest rates, which were raised as part of the adjustment programme. Loan interest rates have averaged over 25 per cent per annum over the last five years. Mortgage rates have also increased. As a result, the price of a three-bedroomed house in a typically middle-class suburb in 1990 was nearly one million Jamaican dollars (about US$150,000). The prices for one-bedroomed apartments currently begin at about J$600,000 (about US$30,000.) The average university graduate earning about J$50,000 following graduation can hardly expect to be able to purchase even the most basic of homes. The situation facing the average worker is much worse.

House rents have increased to such an extent that most lower-income families are forced to sub-let even the most dilapidated, poorly maintained house. As a result, there has been a rise in the number of 'squatters' who have built homes on illegally acquired land, in contravention of established building codes. Since the Government has considerable difficulty providing for housing needs, particularly of the low-income groups, this approach to satisfying housing needs has had to be condoned.

Transportation

Adjustment policies affect the transport sector in a number of ways. For example, with devaluation the costs of imported motor vehicles, fuel and spare parts increase. Fewer people are able to afford the cost of purchasing and maintaining motor cars. This now places pressure on the public transportation system. However, public transport is affected by the cutbacks in government expenditure and the increased cost of buses; thus, the number of available bus seats may actually decline while the demand for them is increasing.

The adjustment policies have affected the Jamaican transport sector in the above-mentioned ways. The cost and availability of both private and public transport has been problematic. The cheapest car on the Jamaican market – the Russian made Lada – retailed recently at J$90,000 (about US$13,000). The distributors of this vehicle have a waiting list of over one thousand orders, with some people still on the list who placed an order over two years ago. The shortage of cars has led to increased prices in the second-hand market, with 15-year-old cars being sold for over J$45,000 (US$7,000).

Alongside this shortage of cars, the public transportation system is chaotic. By official estimates, there is a thirty per cent shortage of bus seats in the capital and its environs. Illegal bus operators known as 'robots' are running a profitable business because of this shortage.

In general, most of the buses are poorly maintained. They are also usually very overcrowded and operate under very inadequate, unpredictable schedules. Workers dependent on public transport lose time and energy travelling on the buses with serious consequences for their productivity. Students using public transport invariably arrive at school either late or so physically exhausted that their first few school hours are virtually wasted.

During 1989, bus fares for adults increased by about 20 per cent. Those for children in school uniform increased by 10 per cent during the year. The fare for children is half that of an adult.

There are no specialised busing facilities for children, and as such, they are usually carried as 'passengers of last resort', after the profitable adult fares have been collected. Shouts of 'no schoolers' by bus crews are widely used to indicate that particular buses do not transport school children.

It has become evident that the effects of debt and poverty on the lives of the poor cannot be effectively countered by individual approaches and actions. More and more, community groups assisted by local NGOs are co-operating to provide for their basic needs and to make demands on the Government for social amenities and community facilities.

Changes in the levels and composition of government expenditure

In response to IMF/World Bank conditionalities related to fiscal restraints, many developing countries have been forced to reduce levels of government expenditure. Most of this reduction has tended to be in what the IMF/World Bank term 'non-productive' services – mainly public health, education and housing. In addition, subsidies which are provided by government to these sectors are eliminated, causing increased charges to be passed on to those using them. The consequence is that poorer people are no longer able to benefit from these services. Stabilisation and structural adjustment programmes have also encouraged increasing privatisation of social services, and this has also had the effect of significantly increasing prices, and thereby denying access to the poorest.

There has been a marked deterioration in the quality of public services provided in the health, education and housing sectors in Jamaica over the last decade. Social services expenditure peaked during the mid-1970s under the PNP government. As a percentage of GDP, social services expenditure fell from 14.5 in 1979 to 4.0 in 1985. Diminished social services have resulted mainly from government fiscal austerity measures associated with adjustment programmes.

Recurrent expenditures on social services such as health and education have been drastically reduced. Investment in social infrastructure such as the building of new schools and hospitals has contracted, while necessary maintenance of social facilities is minimal. Adjustment measures in the 1980s and early 1990s have also led to the introduction of fees for hitherto free services in education and hospitals.

Health

Historically, Jamaica's public health care system, upon which most of the population rely, compared favourably with the best in developing countries. There are at present 24 hospitals and about 350 health centres, with each parish having at least one public hospital and nearly 20 health centres. The health sector presently employs over 10,000 workers.

However, over the last decade, the sector has shown a rapid decline. Total expenditure on health as a percentage of total Government expenditure fell from an average of over 9 per cent in the mid-1970s to just over 5 per cent in 1986-88. Although both recurrent and capital expenditure on health services declined, the decline in capital expenditure was more pronounced. Capital expenditure reductions meant that vital equipment used in the hospitals and health centres could not be replaced. Reduced recurrent expenditures led to inadequate maintenance of facilities, unavailability of supplies including medicines, and less funding for salaries of medical personnel.

The most recent Economic and Social Survey of Jamaica (1989), published by the Planning Institute of Jamaica, clearly states that:

> ...Underfinancing of the health sector continued to affect adversely the provision and delivery of good quality health care. In some critical areas output was reduced and the quality of medical care suffered because of inadequacy of the infrastructure, diagnostic and support services. The attrition of manpower in critical areas of the service continued.

The public health sector has been seriously affected by the loss of personnel at all levels. The public sector doctor/population ratio moved from one doctor for every 2,700 persons in 1971 to one for every 3,000 in 1980, with the latest figure being one for every 5,200. The ratio of nursing personnel to population declined from one nurse for every 540 Jamaicans in 1975 to one nurse for every 1,172 persons in 1985.

With reduced public expenditure on health which has led to deteriorating working conditions in the sector, there has been widespread resignation of health personnel. Coupled with layoffs which have also arisen due to contractions in government funding, the public health sector is now faced with a situation where nearly 30 per cent of all posts were not filled as at June, 1989. Nearly one out of every five posts for physicians was vacant, about one out of every three for registered nurses could not be filled, while over half of the number of pharmacist posts were vacant. Attempts have recently been made to deal with some of the personnel shortages via increases in salaries and allowances for various categories of health personnel. Nurses' salaries were doubled to J$40,000 per annum in 1990 (just under US$6,000 at the prevailing exchange rate), plus allowances. Hourly or sessional rates for all nurses have also been increased.

As part of the adjustment programme, the government has since the mid-80s introduced policies geared towards improving the health sector's performance. Firstly, as part of a 'rationalisation' programme, some hospital wards and many clinics were closed or downgraded. This has resulted in an actual decline in the number of public hospital beds available. Secondly, new fees were implemented in 1984 as part of a programme to cover more of the costs of public health care; this must have seriously disadvantaged poor people who rely heavily on these services. Thirdly, support for privatising the health sector has been provided and as a result the number of private hospitals and clinics is increasing, and these charge market rates for the services provided. Fourthly, a programme for recruiting nurses in Commonwealth countries, including the UK has been introduced; additionally, incentives are being provided locally to attract more school-leavers into nursing.

Some of the policies introduced have increased the suffering of the poor who rely mainly on public health facilities. With reduced public health care, increased fees for these deteriorating services, and more widely available but more costly private health care, poor people find it much more difficult to get access to these services. However, given the poor quality of public health care, SLC figures show that 4 out of every 10 persons in the lowest income group are forced to use private medical care where the cost per visit averages at J$56 (1989) compared to J$4 for public hospital care. The situation is similar with respect to the purchase of medicines as only three out of every ten in the poorest group purchased medicines from public sources. However, over eight of every ten in this group could not buy all the medications prescribed due the prohibitive costs.

Education

Education expenditures are of crucial importance for developing countries, which suffer from shortages of skilled manpower. An uneducated work force is not capable of mastering the most advanced technology and its productivity is severely hampered; thus its output becomes uncompetitive when compared to other countries. In addition, it is estimated that the returns on educational spending, particularly in primary schools, are usually greater than the returns on physical capital expenditure.

Education has historically been the responsibility of the public sector. Less than five per cent of school places at the primary and secondary are provided by private schools. About 600,000 students aged between three and seventeen years old attend over two thousand schools serviced by about 20,000 teachers. Up to the mid-1970s, the overall performance of the education sector in Jamaica compared favourably with countries at similar levels of development. Since then, however, there has been a marked decline in the quality of education.

As a percentage of GDP, government expenditure on education declined from over ten per cent in the 1970s to under five per cent in 1985. At the same time, public expenditure on education fell from nearly 18 per cent of total public expenditure in 1975 to 10.8 per cent in 1984. On the capital expenditure side the situation has been even more serious; capital expenditure on education, which includes the construction of school buildings, installation of laboratory equipment and so on, declined from an annual average of nearly ten per cent of total government capital spending in 1974 to less than one per cent in 1986.

The implications of the cuts in public expenditure on the quality of education are serious. Both primary and secondary schools are very overcrowded as a result of inadequate classroom space. Many schools lack an adequate water supply

Spending on education has been drastically reduced as part of structural adjustment packages to cut government expenditure, and schools are now chronically short of teaching materials.

and sanitation facilities are extremely poor. Textbooks are not available to most students because of their prohibitive costs. With reduced government expenditure on education, working conditions in schools have deteriorated significantly. With teaching materials generally unavailable, and with real incomes of teachers declining, there has been a high rate of attrition in the profession. Many teachers are involved in the informal economy at various levels in an attempt to improve their declining living standards.

Many schools, including some of the 'top' secondary schools, have had to rely on various techniques to mobilise funds to help meet the shortfall in money provided by government. These have included requests for financial assistance from parents, and the holding of various commercial events such as fairs and parties to help top up teachers' salaries and provide for other areas of both recurrent and capital expenditure.

The poorer strata in the society are generally more seriously affected by this deteriorating educational provision. The SLC shows that in the age group three to five years, children in the bottom 20 per cent of Jamaican households are twice as likely as those in the top 20 per cent not to be enrolled in school. The situation is closely similar throughout the entire school system.

Since the majority of poorer children terminate their schooling in primary schools, the situation in primary schools warrants additional scrutiny. Enrolment in primary schools declined during the 1980s by about seven per cent over the period, while there has been an increase in the numbers of children of primary school age in the population. At the same time the number of primary school teachers has also fallen to such an extent that the teacher/pupil ratio has actually worsened in spite of falling numbers of students. There are also high levels of grade repetition and school dropouts at this level.

The SLC data is revealing:

- Over 60 per cent of the poorer strata children abandon mainly primary school between grades seven and nine;
- about one in every four primary schools students cited financial reasons for non-attendance at schools;
- over one in five primary school students have repeated a year more than once;
- the mean annual expenses per child in primary school were J$1119 (1989), with over 60 per cent of this being for 'lunch', and nearly 25 per cent for 'fees'.

What is even more alarming is the suggestion, from usually reliable sources, that over half of the children completing primary school are 'functionally illiterate.'

For Jamaica as a whole, secondary education has shown remarkable deterioration. Mainly as a result of the problems we have outlined above, secondary school performance is marked by low attendance levels and low achievement levels. Data available for total entries and passes for the GCE 'O' levels reveal clearly the seriously worsening situation in the secondary schools. Total number of both entries and passes have been declining. Whereas in 1975, over 7,000 students took the English Language examination with a pass rate of nearly sixty per cent, by 1989, the comparable figures were 5,747 with only 34.5 per cent passes. In English Literature, both the numbers and pass rates have fallen significantly. Pass rates for Economics/ Accounts, Mathematics, Physics, Chemistry and Biology have also dropped.

With respect to the Caribbean Examination Council (CXC), examinations which are replacing GCE examinations in the Caribbean, the pattern has been no different. For example, the pass rates in both English Language and English Literature have both declined over the last two years, as have Economics/Accounts and Mathematics pass rates.

2.6 Fighting back: two responses to material deprivation

With increasing levels of unemployment, deteriorating real incomes, and generally worsening living conditions in Jamaica, people have responded in a variety of ways. Two examples are given in this section.

One widely used response has been migration. Between 1975 and 1980, migration rates averaged about over forty per cent of the natural population decrease annually as many people, especially those with professional and technical qualifications, left Jamaica because of the perceived 'communist threat'. Between 1981 and 1985, however, the migration rates had declined to under 20 per cent of the decrease annually. However,

Emigration is a positive response by individuals to worsening living conditions, but is draining the country of skilled personnel. Waiting outside the US Embassy in Kingston.

NEIL COOPER AND JAN HAMMOND/OXFAM

as adjustment policies leading to worsening living conditions began to have an effect, from around 1986 migration rates climbed to 49 per cent in 1986, 77 per cent in 1987, and 88 per cent in 1988. According to the Economic and Social Survey (1991), 24,600 Jamaicans emigrated in 1990, more than double the 1989 figure of 10,400. On average more than 8 out of every ten legal migrants from Jamaica go to the US, with the remainder to Canada and the UK. As might be expected, at least one in every five migrants is a skilled worker whose departure leaves a significant vacuum in the country's labour market. There is also a significant amount of reported illegal migration to the US from Jamaica.

Another strategy which is used by a number of Jamaicans is participation in the informal economy. Informal economic activity is defined to include those which violate laws or official regulations, or contravene generally accepted standards and codes of business behaviour. Illegal activities fall within the informal economy and these have shown some increases in the 1980s.

Empirical studies show that the informal economy in Jamaica has been growing and its size is estimated at over 60 per cent of the size of the formal or reported economy. Those activities in the informal economy which are legal have been increasing; many of these operations are categorised as micro-enterprises or for some even 'pre-micro' businesses. Most recent estimates indicate over 30,000 of these operating in Jamaica.

2.7 Alternative adjustment policies

The poor in Jamaica, as in many developing countries, face tremendous material deprivation and significant threats to their well-being when their governments are engaged in IMF/World Bank adjustment programmes. It is impossible and would border on arrogance for any one individual to compile an alternative approach which a country should follow in order to overcome its economic and social problems. This must come from the majority of the people themselves. However, we make a few suggestions in the paragraphs which follow.

Policies to reduce the debt servicing burden warrant some

consideration. External debt policies can be classified firstly, into those which completely eliminate the debt payments, and secondly, those which reduce the payments to tolerable levels.

Among the first group are included conscious debt repudiation or default where the borrowing country unilaterally decides against repayment; such a decision is very risky and could lead to retaliatory measures such as termination of all credit or an economic embargo by creditor countries and institutions. Such actions could seriously jeopardise the economy of the debtor country. Alternatively, debt 'forgiveness' may allow the debtor country to cease debt repayment because the lending country has 'written off' outstanding debts; it is to be noted that this is possible only with respect to bilateral arrangements.

Among the second group of proposals are included debt rescheduling where the repayment periods are extended; the limitation of debt service payments to a certain percentage of export earnings; and the conversion of debt into equity.

Canada recently 'forgave' a portion of debts owed to it by a number of countries, Jamaica included; and Jamaica has managed to reschedule all of its commercial bank debts.

In our view, the current structural adjustment programmes in which Jamaica is involved should be changed in order to reduce the adverse impact on the country's poor. What is required is a 'pro-poor' modification of existing IMF/World Bank policies. This may include some or all of the following; firstly, any further public expenditure cutbacks should ensure that those expenditures which benefit poor people are retained. Where already reduced, previous expenditure levels should be reinstated. Secondly, those subsidies which can lead to worsening of the well-being of poor people should not be reduced, while those which have already been eliminated must be re-introduced. Thirdly, measures should be implemented to help those workers who have been made redundant as a result of adjustment policies; policies which can stimulate increases in demand for such labour can be encouraged. Redundant workers could be provided with small amounts of low interest, start-up capital for micro-business ventures.

Over the medium term, the Jamaican authorities should devise policy prescriptions geared towards promoting development for

This motor mechanic runs her own business, but small-scale entrepreneurs find it hard to get credit. Government policies which encouraged small businesses could boost the economy.

the majority. These policies ought to reflect a concern for redistribution, social equality, and popular participation in decision making. In this context, priority concerns will be deliberate, conscious, and planned attacks on poverty.

In dealing with the poor, a basic-needs strategy should be devised. This strategy has as its main foci the personal needs of the people such as food, clothing and housing, and the broader public needs such as health care, education, sanitation, and culture. In our view, employment policies are critical in facilitating the adequate satisfaction of the basic needs of the Jamaican people.

The institutional arrangements are also critical. In our view, total reliance on the market mechanism is problematic. The private sector, by itself, cannot facilitate development in the interest of the wider society. The state has a role to play in economic and social development. It should, however, not serve narrow minority social and economic interests since this generates class polarisation and social instability. Concern for the majority of the Jamaican people should guide public policy and as such, every possible attempt should be made to ensure that there is equity and social justice in the distribution of the costs and benefits of adjustment.

In our policy proposal, there is a useful role for non-governmental organisations. Many NGOs have developed strong links with important pressure groups resisting those policies which impact negatively on the poor. Two of the main strengths of NGOs in Jamaica are their capacity to help service those poor communities which have been neglected by government services and their generally acceptable approach geared towards generating self-confidence, capacity, and organisational capability among the poorer groups in the society.

In the latter context, NGOs can play a vital role in re-introducing various participatory forms like self-help and co-operative arrangements which have been eliminated during the period of IMF/World Bank adjustment. By their nature of their operations, Jamaican NGOs are well placed to help reduce the dependence of various community groups and organisations on external funding by generating self-help programmes and projects.

ALISON BROWNLIE/OXFAM

Farming family on their smallholding. Farmers face steeply rising costs for inputs, and problems in marketing their produce.

3

Interviews

These interviews were conducted by James Ferguson in October 1991.

The small farmer

Uriah Williams has a small piece of land in a village in St James parish. He and his wife, Millicent, also make craft items for sale to tourists on the north coast. They used to have a stall at the Montego Bay market and are now participating in a communal farm project in their village.

Farming is a little slow at the moment. We don't have the cash to move along, so we have to find other ways of making a living. We've just started up as a group, and we have about half an acre. That area is a captured [squatted] section of land, so we're waiting for authority from the government to use it. I do a little farming around my house for myself. I plant bananas, sweetsops, soursops, and other fruit like mangoes and pears. We eat most of it ourselves and give some away. We don't take such small amounts to the market. What we are expecting to grow on the joint farm will be to sell in the market. There are other farmers who'll be working with us. We'll be raising cows and goats. I used to live in Manchester and did a lot of farming there. But when I moved over to St James, I did a different sort of farming, on the hills, near Maroon Town. That was an area where there's a lot of rain and you can grow anything. Here, you have to put in short crops such as callaloo, red peas, peanuts and cabbage. You can grow a little banana, too, but you have to have water from the pipe to water it since we don't get a lot of rainfall.

We used to have a little shop in the market in Montego Bay. One of our bigger girls looked after it. She made the things and took them there to sell. But there was too much competition, everybody had the same things. So we had to find another way out, making things like belts, tams, rugs and toys. We're trying to sell these items to tourists.

Sometimes for days on end we didn't sell anything in the market. So I had to go out and look for a few days' work. Sometimes I do some masonry or chop wood. Sometimes I even buy bottles, Desnoes and Geddes or Coca-Cola, and I put them on my head and carry them to the depot and sell them. At the factory they pay 20 dollars for a crate of 24 empties. I pay four dollars per dozen, so I don't make anything much. It might take most of the morning to do that. If I could get a little van I could go further around and sell the bottles in Kingston, where you get a better price. Sometimes when you can't get any work, you can't bring any money home. Other times, you might get 400 dollars. This is how we get our wages, not by the week, but by doing occasional jobs for 100 or 200 dollars. So in a week you might have 200 dollars to feed the children and send them to school.

You have to pinch and cut all the time. It's tough. We mostly buy rice and flour and a little sugar. We hardly ever buy meat any more, perhaps chicken once a week. Chicken costs 15 dollars a pound and fish is 30 dollars, so we eat a lot of vegetables that we grow at home like beans and peas. I don't drink or smoke. The bigger folks can buy a crate of drinks, but the poor people have to leave that aside. We eat enough to keep alive, but the children would like to have more milk and cheese. They need more vitamins and protein from things like fish. One of our children is giving us problems with her health. She has stomach cramps all the time, sometimes she's sick when she eats, maybe she can't stand the hunger.

We have to spend most of our earnings on the children. We pay 240 dollars to the Secondary and 90 dollars for the little one. And we have to pay for their books. A book is 130 or 150, and every year they need a new one as they go into a different class. If they're sick, we take them to the local clinic. Now it costs 35 dollars for an adult and 25 for a child to register. Then there are different prices for all the medicines when you get sent to the pharmacy. The hospital is so rough now that everyone's afraid to go there.

There's never been a good time for poor people in Jamaica. It was better in the 1970s, when the government was doing some things for poor people. A lot of people are blaming the present government for the debt problem, but I think you should blame the people who took the money and spent it. We have to honour our debts. Each of us, each little baby now owes something like two thousand dollars. That is why things keep going up. Not even half of the people got any of the money. It went into different areas to suit other people's purposes. Borrowing to help everybody is fine. But when it just goes to certain people and for yourself, that's no good.

When [hurricane] Gilbert blew, we didn't get any help, we had to help ourselves. I had a three-apartment house which burned down completely in 1982. I never got a cent to help me rebuild my home. I had to take my axe and cut stone to build it again, and until now no government has helped me. On the day the hurricane came we were down in the market. We had to rush home, and there was water right through the house, we had to sweep all the mud out of the house. But we were so lucky that our house was made of concrete. We were safe inside, but the windows and doors blew in. The other houses that were made of wood were destroyed. Gilbert just took the zinc roofs and tossed them to and fro. The government helped a few of those people. But the majority of people who really should have been helped didn't get anything. When the zinc came, the people who were handing it out gave it to their own friends. Some of the bigger ones took it to make fences, but the poor people whose houses blew down didn't get any. There were also building stamps, to buy materials with. But you had to be on the right side politically to get them.

I think helping the small farmer is the best way out of Jamaica's difficulties. But after the promises it takes so long for anything to happen that you get frustrated. Farming without proper transportation for the crops doesn't make any sense. The roads here are terrible. The crops are there perishing, and you can't get them into town. I would like to see the government help the idle boys and girls on the street to get jobs. We need more factories. Even if the government built a glass factory, for instance, in Montego Bay, that would help a lot. You could teach the young people how to make bottles and other things.

So many things are imported that we can make or grow here. We can grow red peas, onions, tomato, Irish potato here, yet they import a lot of these things. Take banana, for example. The ones that aren't up to the mark for exporting should be used here. You could open a factory to make flour or chips or anything. I believe that would be much better, and people would get more work. But now when you take your truckload of bananas to the depot, they reject a lot of them. That's no good for the farmers, they can only eat a few hands of the rejected ones and they have to dump them. So the farmers get vexed, cut down the banana and try to plant other crops. But when the other crops come, it's the same thing, they don't have any market. Why don't we tin things like carrot or breadfruit? We should have a tinning factory, then we could tin vegetables and juices and ship them away like that.

Everything's in Kingston. We don't have any cold storage here for bananas or potatoes. The cement factory is there, so when a truck has to go there to collect cement you have to pay double the price for it.

Some Jamaicans are leaving now just to make an adequate living. Staying in Jamaica makes no sense because our dollar isn't worth anything, so you have to go where you can get a bigger dollar. It's only a few people who can do that, the majority have to stay here and survive.

I believe that the floating of the dollar should be stopped. There should be a steady rate. The black market always brings the dollar up, so that even the government can't get the money to do its business. If I had one American dollar now and I can get twenty for it on the black market rather than the official rate, don't you think I would go for the higher rate? That's how the black market is. You can always find a man out there who'll give you more than the banks. But this is tearing down the country, because the government can't get the American dollars to import the things we need. We have to get things like oil and wheat – things we don't produce here.

I was born in 1932, I'm nearly sixty. You get an old-age pension when you're sixty-two, I think. It's something like sixty dollars a month. I think you don't get it in cash, but in food stamps. You go to certain shops and you change them for supplies. As you can see, it can be pretty tough.

The health workers

Luris Gayle, Delzie Murray, Donna Kerr and Hyacinth Allen are community and health workers, involved in some of the most depressed areas of St James parish. The communities they deal with suffer from a lack of basic facilities and services, such as sanitation, safe water and preventive health care. They are also badly affected by high levels of unemployment.

Health is a very big problem under the current circumstances. It's something we face every day. People are unable to finance themselves when it comes to medication. So they have to live on the mercy of other people, or they die. There's hardly any medication in the hospitals, so if you go to the doctor you have to find the money to buy your own medication. If you can't find the money, you know what is going to happen to you!

Most of the kids in the depressed areas are malnourished. They are unable to buy the basic things such as food. Most homes are run by single parents, and there is a huge amount of unemployment. So you begin to see child labour appearing, because the parents are unable to earn enough to support these children. There are dump areas, where garbage is disposed of, and children will go to those areas to find food, to find bottles to sell to make a living, or other objects to sell or take home.

As community health workers, working in three communities with mothers and children, what we discover among most of these families is that the mother is the head. She finds it very hard to cope with the children. In one of these communities there is the dump, the official dump for the parish, and that's where these children earn their livelihood. Children will stop from school for days. As soon as the garbage truck passes by, they'll run behind and collect what bottles they can. They even eat the stuff from the truck. This makes them sick and they end up in hospital. We have a counselling programme and try to educate the mothers and children about the dangers of the dump. For instance, we know that the water source is very poor. Most likely it's infected with typhoid. So we try to educate them to keep their containers clean and to boil the water. Sanitation is also very important, since these people don't have latrines. We've been trying to show them how to help themselves by digging pits.

ALISON BROWNLIE/OXFAM

**Trained by an Oxfam-supported church organisation, Garnett Poiser now
works in his own community. Oxfam provided funds for latrines like this
one after Hurricane Gilbert.**

The second basic need is really education. Some of the parents
are unable to send the children to school because they're not
working. Some of the children live a long way away from school
and so need money for transportation. They also need lunch
money and they can't afford it. Some do not want to go because
they can't read or write, they didn't get a good start.

There's also the problem of nutrition. The St James health
department has given us food supplements, but we don't just
give them out. We also try to educate the people about how to
prepare meals. Because many of these people hardly want to
listen when you're talking to them, not that they are unwilling
to, but their biggest need is that they're hungry. They need the
food, so we try to get the message across as well as feeding
them. We try to get help for them in many different areas. We go

to the Children's Service Division, which deals with children who are being abused, who are not in school, and we try to get them back into school and to get the families together.

There's one area I would really like to emphasise, and that's the lack of housing. Because of the debt crisis, you find that people have to live in rented houses and then they go and capture land so that they can build houses. Now when they go and capture this piece of land and they start to put up a little shack with zinc roof and whatever, that's when the sanitation problem starts. They don't have the money at the same time to build a latrine.

The housing situation is getting much worse. There are still a lot of houses available, but the poor people cannot afford them, not even the low-income housing. That is why most people squat, capturing a piece of land and building a little shack on it. But they're afraid to spend their money to put in important things like toilets because they say 'we only captured the land, we only want a room'. Sometimes if the land is being sold to private interests, they'll be pushed off anyway. But if it's really government land they may be there for years and years. In some areas that we work in, the land is being surveyed, cut up and people are now about to pay, a little at a time. But some people, on the other hand, 'capture' land which is right in the tourist areas, on the sea-front. The private people there do not tolerate them, because they put up shacks and it depreciates the value of the land.

My community is on private land, owned by several families. Some are here and some are abroad. And the people have asked several times for the government to come and buy it, but I don't know if they'll do it. The main problem we have over there is sanitation. We also have a few malnourished children and a lot of unemployment. The young boys are prone to drugs and the young girls to pregnancies. This is one of the most depressed communities and people have very low self-esteem. Because of the name of the community over the years, people are afraid to move out and seek jobs, because they say 'nobody will look at us or listen to us'. So they're in a little world by themselves. And if people do move out and get educated, they want to move to another community or abroad rather than going back and building it up.

But you shouldn't get the idea that people from that community aren't talented or gifted. It's just that they need help, and when they go out into the wider community people just don't want to accept them. Crime and drugs have given them a bad name. But working in the community, I've realised that if you motivate them, they'll work as well as anybody. They just need a chance. Recently we've built seven latrines. It might not be much, it might be just the tip of the iceberg, but things are happening. And government, through the Health Department, is doing what it can. They are monitoring by sending public health inspectors, nurses and nutritionists who work alongside us. The public health nurses do immunisation, the inspectors do sanitation, shops inspection, food handling, that sort of thing. The programme is making progress.

The crisis will never get better until we stop borrowing. People will have to learn how to become more self-reliant, more self-sufficient. Only that will help them. And if the people decide that we don't want the IMF any more, and we want to develop on what we have, it can get better, it can change. But with the IMF, I don't see a way out. Many of the things we need, like foodstuffs, we can produce right here. We have a lot of resources. We have a lot of people who just sit around doing nothing because we cannot pay them. We also have the land.

We need to export more to other Caribbean countries as well as the big countries. We have a lot of tropical fruits, for instance, and when it's the season there's an abundance and often they go to waste. We don't can enough, we don't export enough. We have an abundance of pineapples, mangoes, oranges. If we could export more of what we grow, that would make life a little more bearable since almost every Jamaican person produces some fruit or another. I think we want to export, but the IMF comes in with so many specifications. They say 'you have to import our apples and grapes, onions and so on'. So they are clamping down on our exports and saying 'take our things, we want our money'.

Participation is a problem. One political party builds up, then the other one comes in for five years and destroys what was being built up. People need to participate more, not to just look after their own concerns. If we can learn to share more, to get involved, we can get on.

The church worker

Mike James is the sub-regional co-ordinator of the Caribbean Conference of Churches in Jamaica. Religion plays a very important part in the lives of most Jamaicans, and there are a large number of different denominations present on the island. The Caribbean Conference of Churches, an ecumenical grouping of churches throughout the region, has adopted an outspoken position against the structural adjustment programmes in force in the Caribbean.

It's really pointless to have debt rescheduling while at the same time you're increasing your debt burden and you're adding new debt on top of the old. In fact, we were at one point in a position where the interest on the loans we already had was higher than the new loans we were getting. You might as well stop the whole thing at that point, when you're paying out more than you're getting in.

The frightening thing that we're seeing here in Jamaica, and in the rest of the Third World, is that you cannot put a face onto the oppression. Now it's just the rule of the market. It's not ideological any more; there's no wicked capitalist over here, or communist over there, no individuals as such. It's just the way the market is. It's some sort of rule of supply and demand. You can do nothing about it, and that is the frightening thing. You have increasing frustration and poverty, but people have no way of identifying anybody as culpable. It's all been very much depoliticised.

The situation in the public hospital, for example, is really grim. The last time I was down there, the doctors were going out to the corner shop to buy spirits because there was no medical alcohol available for operations. Those services which are supposed to be the right of the population as a whole are getting very bad indeed. Education for the poor in Jamaica has always been an escape valve. It provides the escape valve through which the brightest of the poor have been able to advance. Increasingly, as the education system collapses, and it becomes even narrower, even that possibility of escape for the poor is being cut off. Because there's such a gap between the children in the public schools and those who can afford to pay. At Peter and Paul, a private church school, you have to pay 2,000 dollars a term, fees have gone up by 40 per cent. Compare that to how it is with a minimum wage. And when it comes to the Common Entrance exam, where you have 50,000 children competing for 5,000 places, Peter and Paul school gets 98 per cent of its pupils in. The whole system of school inspectors that used to exist has completely collapsed. So that there is the whole phenomenon of street children, and large numbers of children are simply not in the education system at all. No parent would be prosecuted for not sending children to school, there's no room in the system for them. So the number of illiterates is increasing.

In the 1960s and 1970s there was at least the expectation that the goal of universal primary education was attainable. Now, it seems as though we're giving up on that. Teachers and nurses are being recruited by American schools and hospitals. So it's a vicious circle, where you have limited resources for training people and those who do get trained are faced with such dreadful conditions that the temptation to emigrate is really very powerful. It's a very difficult situation for the country.

Really, the Jamaican government is not running the economy any longer. It's the IMF and the World Bank. So, it becomes a dreadful escape from responsibility on the part of our governments. Whereas in the 1960s and 1970s they felt, and we expected, that they would be in charge of the economy. now they no longer are...and they're saying that. Rightly or wrongly, they're saying 'we're in receivership to the donor nations, and they really make the decisions about our economy'.

To be honest, the churches here are playing less of a role than in Latin America, but increasingly they are moving away from the old Protestant ethic that says if you borrow money, you have to pay it back. We're beginning to see the issue of debt, of debt rescheduling and even debt write-off as a moral issue. Some of us really cringe when we hear leaders of the wealthy countries talk about 'debt forgiveness'. It's interesting how the wealthy are now beginning to use theological terms! A concept such as forgiveness which used to be the prerogative of God now gets taken on by those who out of their munificence and bounty are able to forgive debt. Here, when they start taking over theological language is precisely the moment when the churches should say 'wait a minute, if you're talking about forgiveness, who has to do the forgiving?' Remember Columbus and all the rest of it! We had a big meeting of church leaders from Latin America and the Caribbean here last year on the foreign debt, and we called for the churches to take a united position on the moral issues surrounding the injustices of debt. Particularly in terms of who has benefited from the debt and who has paid. And also in terms of trying to build up, not only at the national level but also at the regional level, the kind of solidarity that doesn't exist between governments in the South. When they try to establish any kind of solidarity they're immediately pounced on by those nations who themselves always deal with individual debtor countries as the 'Paris Club'! Here is where the regional church can, and increasingly does, play an important role.

The issue is not something that would naturally and traditionally come onto the churches' agenda. But increasingly the CCC and some individual churches are taking a lead. There's still a lot more to do. Particularly in rural areas, where in many cases the church is the one community institution with any credibility, there's a much more important role to be played in terms of educating and helping people to understand. We have access to the media, particularly to phone-in programmes which are very popular. But even within the churches, there's this dreadful sense of helplessness, a feeling of 'what can we do?'

One of the criticism that was made of our recent video is that we're not really coming forward with alternatives to the debt crisis. Maybe more has to be done on that, but our own perspective is that the whole process of discovering solutions comes from a dialogue with the people at the base, who themselves have something to say in terms of what the solutions might be. I don't know if that's a cop-out in the absence of clear solutions. What we want to stress, though, is the regional nature of the problem. The situation in the Dominican Republic, for instance, is just a carbon copy of what is happening here in Jamaica.

How are people surviving? If the middle classes are really finding it hard to manage, how do people on the minimum wage cope when bus fares go up by 50 per cent?

What is dreadful about the so-called debt-for-equity swaps is that you can't restrict it. You come under pressure from investors

Sugar workers taking part in an open-air church service. Religion plays an important part in Jamaican life, and now the churches are beginning to become more politically aware.

coming in to buy up Jamaican real estate and hotels and so on, excluding locals who don't have foreign exchange. You just end up selling your country to outsiders coming in. We've just privatised the Jamaica Telephone Company, and local investors could not buy into it because hard cash was needed to meet the IMF's next monthly payment. So the foreign investors made a killing, because they knew even better than the local investors how badly the government needed the money and that they'd sell it for a song. They're planning to sell off Air Jamaica as well, and the outsiders are expecting it to be almost given away. It's not that we want to exclude foreign investment, we just don't want to sell off the country.

The Free Trade Zone workers

Lloyd O'Connor, Joan Creighton, Doreen Hall, Sharon Grey, Una Young and Myrtle Lewinson are all former workers in the Free Trade Zones in Kingston and Montego Bay. The Free Trade Zones offer foreign companies attractive tax exemptions to set up offshore assembly plants, exporting clothing and electrical goods to the US and European markets. Wages are notoriously low.

....I used to work for a company down in the Free Zone. They only employed men, about 120 of us. We made switches and plugs. In a week we put out about 60,000 switches. The flat rate pay was 180 dollars. We used to start at eight and work through until four. One day they had a sort of opening with the Production Minister and a Member of Parliament. The management said that if we had anything to say to them, we should write a letter and hand it to the management before the official could see it! I couldn't keep smiling because of all the things going on there, so they were planning to fire me. So I just resigned.

....I had a similar experience. We went to work from eight until four thirty. We got a flat rate of 120 dollars. They used to take National Insurance, NIS, but we didn't ever get our NIS card and they took away all that money from the 120 dollars. You also pay income tax and education tax, and after all the deductions we got something like 90 dollars. I worked at Montego Medical, making shorts mostly. They had one or two men, but the majority of workers were women.

....I used to work at XL Garments, over in Trelawny. The owner was a Jamaican, and at one point he needed financial help and went into partnership with a Canadian firm. That was when we had to start work at seven-thirty. At first it was seven o'clock, but we got together and said no, we couldn't start at that time because some of us lived miles away from the factory. This Canadian firm came in and taught us a lot about production. We appreciated that. They also recognised who the people were who were prepared to speak up on behalf of the other workers, so they would appoint them as supervisors. They tried to bring you into the management structure so that you would keep your big

Workers leaving the Free Trade Zone, Kingston.

mouth shut! There were workers who were on a piece rate, like a dollar and ten cents for ten pieces. Some workers were lazy and would just go home with 90 to 100 dollars. When all the taxes were deducted from the 100 dollars, you might end up with 48 or 50 dollars. You have workers who cry out at that point. But management would say, if you can't accept that, we'll close the factory, you go home and we'll see how you survive. Trade unions are not allowed. Any plant under the 807 and JAMPRO programme [Free Trade Zone government schemes] doesn't allow trade unions. If you don't like it, you have to get out.

....I started working in the Free Zone for 120 dollars per week. I was doing quality checking. You check and you check all day long. We were doing shorts and I had to check hundreds of pairs each day, looking inside at the elastic and the stitching. The people on the line would curse us if we sent shorts back for repair. They wanted to kill us! At the same time, the management were saying 'we need better quality, we've got to have quality'. We got a ten-minute break, and as soon as you got a cup of tea or soup you had to go back. Sometimes you had to throw it away. Lunch was half an hour, and you had to stand in a line to buy your own lunch, since they provided nothing. You had to pay your own transport fares as well, and when the prices go up you just have to pay in order to reach your work. If you're late, they send you home, they clock you out, they say 'listen, don't bother, go home'. So you have to start at twelve o'clock and you miss half a day's pay. You just have to be here, it doesn't matter how far you're coming from. If there's a day when you have a transportation problem, they say 'it's not our problem'. If your machine breaks down, you have to stay an extra half hour. People faint over their machines sometimes, it's so hot and full of dust. People start having problems with their nerves, they start going to the doctor every month. There's a lady they call 'the pharmacy' because she's always got her bottle of pills. You're expected to be a hundred per cent worker, and if they find five defective pieces in a day from you they put it on a graph. If the graph goes down below a certain point, they say you're not needed any more because you're not a hundred per cent worker. There's no future in all that. I couldn't stay.

....My last experience was in June. I did what they call on-line auditing. I was like a slave-driver, so they paid me 200 dollars a week. But I had to stand for the eight hours I worked. It's like misery. You have to turn the garment right around, and management said you can't sit down to do that. So I had to stand. When one foot was tired I stood on the other one, then that one began to burn. When you go to the bathroom, you have someone calling you, asking why you're taking so long. There were three of us doing the on-line auditing and a fourth woman who was in charge of us. She always found more faults than we did, so management would complain to us, saying why hadn't we found as many faults as her? If we did find faults, the workers would be mad at us, because we had to send back a whole box with as many as twelve bundles to be done again. I couldn't take the pressure, so I left.

....The worst thing right now is the high prices. Take milk, for example. Condensed or powdered milk is essential if you have children, to make porridge and other things. A pack of milk used to cost 50 cents, now it's four dollars, and a tin of milk used to be 5.50 but now it's 10.50 at the lowest. So when you go the supermarket at the weekend your little pay can't buy much. By

Monday or Tuesday you don't have anything left. You're frustrated, you don't know who to turn to, you don't know what to do. We'll soon be having real malnutrition problems, because our pay just can't buy food any more.

Medicine costs a lot of money. When you go to the hospital you pay to register before the doctor will see you. When you go to casualty you pay, you have to pay for everything – a blood test, an injection, anything. After the doctor has prescribed, you go to the pharmacy. Now maybe you've been prescribed three items and sometimes they give you one, the cheapest one, and they send you to the pharmacy to buy the most expensive ones. Right now I've got two prescriptions in my bag, which are very important for my children, and I can't pay for them.

Housing is a major problem. The houses they're building are called low-income housing, but nobody in our financial situation can have a house like that. Right now they have a housing scheme in an area next door to me. It's supposed to be low-income, but you have to pay 40,000 dollars to get one. You have to do it through the bank, and pay something like 1000 dollars a month. Where would someone who's working for 150 dollars a week get that sort of money? Not even nurses, policemen or teachers can afford that.

The problems really started in the late seventies and early eighties. We started borrowing and depending on borrowing. In the seventies we used to be more self-sufficient. We had a lot of farming. We used to have this company that took the food from the farmers, the AMC. When the other party came in, they closed down the AMC and the farmers got frustrated and stopped planting. So from the seventies through the eighties there's been chaos because of borrowing all that money. We don't know where all that money went. We're not benefiting from the loan.

The young have it worst. Maybe older people are luckier, because their parents might have left them a piece of land or something else. But consider when the parents don't have anything to give to their children. They turn to prostitution or anything like that. They hustle and they thieve. And some kids get hold of ganja and they sell that to get cocaine, and they mix that up with other things and just go crazy. Everyone's just trying to make their bread.

The problems of single mothers

Daphne Binns is a community animator, working specifically with single mothers and their children in an urban area near Montego Bay. Women without skills have been particularly affected by rising food prices and deteriorating social services. The community animation project aims to teach otherwise unskilled women means of self-employment and also to create stronger forms of community organisation which can press for better facilities and services.

Since the 1970s all the governments that have come to power have done so with the support of the poorer class. What they did when they got in, though, was to borrow all this IMF money, and poor people say that they used it to do their personal business. And so the economic crisis keeps getting worse every day. The poorer class tends to suffer more, because, for instance, there's a really serious housing problem in Jamaica, so that people have to go and 'capture' government lands to live on because they can't afford to pay rent. There are no jobs for them.

There needs to be more education about family planning. Many men may have two or three girlfriends and they get them pregnant. Then they move to another area, and the women have to be both mother and father towards the children without any help, and that's very hard for them. So you have a whole lot of unwanted children on the street, who sometimes turn into criminals.

Single mothers like those do day work, wash clothes for other people perhaps. They might make 50 dollars, which isn't enough to buy food, buy clothes or pay the rent. It's really rough. Only God knows how they survive. The programme I'm working in shows them how they can be self-employed, how they can help themselves and their children to go to school. We do dress-making, embroidery, crochet, stuffed toys and all these things. We charge them 10 dollars a month for the training, and what we do with the money is to pay someone to look after the women's children while they're training. Sometimes the women can't find the money, but we don't turn them away. We make them feel just at home as the ones who can pay. We just want them to achieve something.

Most of the women don't work at all. They are totally

dependent on men. They become victims all the time, since the men have control over them, knowing that they depend on them. So they know they'll do whatever they tell them to do. It becomes very miserable and heart-aching, because sometimes they quarrel and then it's the man who leaves, and the woman has to become the bread-winner. Some of the women who are completely abandoned become prostitutes. Their man has left them, they have their children to look after, they don't have a skill, and so they think of a way to get money. They go to the hotel areas, where there are foreigners, and that's how they make their living.

With the new General Consumption Tax there are certain basic items of food in the supermarket where the tax isn't put on, but they still raise the prices. For instance, the poor class in Jamaica cannot do without rice, flour, sugar and cornmeal. Especially those who have a whole lot of children use the cornmeal to make porridge. You also need skimmed milk. You used to get a small packet of skimmed milk powder for 55 cents and it's now four dollars. A tin of milk used to be 2.50, now it's 10.60. A mother of four or five children cannot buy the tinned milk for her children, and she can't even afford the skimmed milk powder. Now there are no controls. The shopkeeper can sell these things for whatever he wants to. If you go to small communities, the shopkeepers there have to go out and buy their goods, and whatever they spend on transport they add to the price of the goods. Cornmeal used to be really cheap. It used to be the only thing that people could run to, to give their children porridge in the morning. Now it's over three dollars a pound. Poor people cannot buy it.

If I took a hundred dollars to the market, what I buy might only last for three days. Rent has gone up, water rates have gone up, the light bill has gone up. It's very hard. If you had a refrigerator you could say 'I'll cook today and serve the same meals today and tomorrow.' But I can't buy a refrigerator which is over 10,000 dollars. And if I cook a little meal today, maybe tomorrow I won't find the money to do the same. So there are a lot of people who go to bed without dinner. That's why you find a lot of thieves. Because people are hungry, they're not just going to sit down and die! They think of how they can get something to eat. If I have a bunch of bananas there, as night comes down it'll just disappear.

The crisis affects women more than men because they carry the burden at all times. A mother cannot disown her child, but a man can. So we are the ones who feel it even more than the men. There may be a few men who really stand up to their responsibilities, but a lot of them just run away and it's the mothers who have to shoulder those problems. So there's a lot of frustration, and sometimes they take it out on the children. A child may say 'my mother's too rough on me' and he goes astray. A lot of children end up on the street, causing problems, and some become criminals. The strains are much more on the mothers. They're the ones who carry a really heavy burden.

I can't really recall a time when things were better. Our parents used to complain about how hard things were. But they weren't as hard as now. Because in those days there were a lot of people who farmed. But nowadays those people are leaving the countryside and going into the town areas, where you have to buy every little thing. If we put more into farming, producing our own food, things would be better. The government is importing the same things as we can produce. If you go into the supermarket, you'll see American red peas there. People leave the local produce and buy that. So we're helping to devalue our dollars, because when we buy foreign things, the government imports more. In the Kingston area there are people who buy imported water from America! The best water you could think of is from Jamaica. If we had fewer imported goods and bought more of our own things that we produce here in Jamaica, we would find that things got better. Our dollar is frazzled right out, it's worth nothing. That's how the black market comes in.

What we need now is more unity. People need to come together more. If you've ever seen crabs in a pan, you'll see how they get together to escape. What they do is they form a line and climb on each other's backs until they reach the top of the pan, and the ones who reach the top pull the other ones up until they're all gone. If we do things like that, we'll find that things get better in our country.

The higgler

Dunstan Whittingham is General Secretary of the Jamaica Vendors,
Higglers and Market Association. This organisation was established in
1986 by traders from the informal sector as a response to the
government's plans to 'clean up' the centre of downtown Kingston. The
Association defends the rights of higglers to trade openly and legally
and stresses their growing importance as the economic crisis drastically
raises consumer prices controlled by the formal sector.

In Jamaica you have a formal sector, like the established stores,
which are downtown, and you have also the banking sector
which is also part of the formal sector. Then you find the
informal sector, made up of higglers who do the trading. There
are higglers, vendors, small traders and informal commercial
importers. The informal commercial importers are mainly people
who go overseas and buy in places like Panama, Curacao, Haiti
and the Cayman Islands, Miami and as far as New York. They
bring back dry goods like clothes, shoes and cosmetics and
sometimes electrical appliances. This has brought about an
increase in the numbers of people involved as distributors and
traders on the sidewalk. We estimate that higglers and vendors
make up about 70 per cent of what is classified as the informal
sector. The small business sector, small entrepreneurs such as
barbers, dressmakers, small club operators and so on, only make
up about 30 per cent.

Over 100,000 people are directly involved in our trade. And a
report has shown that at least 350,000 people are involved
directly or indirectly. You have to consider the informal taximan,
the informal travel service, the informal bag handlers and
cartmen. If you go to the airport, you'll see how many people are
involved, from the customs officials downwards. Higglers
always have big families, too. I've got seven kids, so you can see
how many people depend on the sector. Most people who work
in the trade are women, maybe 65 per cent.

Another side of the trade is the export dimension. The higglers
have been doing a lot of exporting, but in an informal way. We
take in agricultural produce and use the money to buy more
things to bring back. The best place for selling is the Cayman
Islands because of the limited land space and the fact that all food

is imported. We take things like yam and sweet potato. We have farmers who supply us or we go to a wholesale market such as Coronation. We get a very good price in Cayman Island dollars.

You always have people to assist you in the other countries. When our Haitian friends come here we can accommodate them in our homes because often they don't have enough money to stay at a hotel. And when you go there they help you by taking you around. You need assistance, because you might end up walking somewhere you're not meant to and get robbed. In Panama, for instance, the level of theft is very high. But there's more and more crime in all the territories because of the economic situation and high inflation.

Higglering isn't just a Jamaican question, it's a regional and international question. In a country like Brazil, for instance, the GDP isn't created by the private sector, but by the informal sector. In Jamaica the informal sector is becoming more diversified. We are moving into pharmaceuticals and medicines, auto parts and so on. We bring these things in based on orders.

Sometimes there's the problem of competition between the formal sector and the informal sector. They often complain that we're a traffic hazard, preventing pedestrians from moving on the sidewalk, they claim that we create shabbiness with our shacks. They accuse us of dumping cheap goods on Jamaica. But, at the same time, most of us are becoming shoppers for the established merchants. A lot of the goods in their stores aren't obtained by them going overseas but by us supplying them. And this is bringing about an understanding between us as higglers and them as established merchants. So the level of competition gap has now narrowed, since we've turned ourselves into wholesalers. Even including airfares, duties, transportation and everything else, our prices used to be lower than theirs. When we work at the wholesale rate, we make about 33 and a third per cent profit. When we sell our goods on our own we make up to 60 per cent, that's the margin, but that margin includes the time it takes to sell those goods. And we don't have an environment where we have a roof over our head, so the sun burns out the goods, and we have to find some canvas to cover them.

So the wholesaling has helped a lot of people who were unemployed, underemployed or unemployable to find work.

BELINDA COOTE/OXFAM

As unemployment has increased, more and more people are earning their living in the informal sector as street traders.

Neither the government nor the private sector is in a position to create that number of jobs. In this trade there are doctors, lawyers, policemen, soldiers, teachers. They do both their formal work and their informal work, because although they are employed their wage cannot carry them. The flock of higglers you see today comes from unemployment. A big number started with the IMF crisis in the late 1970s when there were a lot of redundancies.

The Tax Compliance Certificate has made it more difficult to get into higglering, but it's brought more decency into the trade, because before almost anyone could get into higglering. You can only obtain foreign exchange from the bank if you have a Tax Compliance Certificate and you need it to clear your goods at the airport. It means that your income tax, your National Insurance, your education tax have to be up to date to the last month. What the government is doing is dragging us in from the informal sector into a formal state. We pay all the same taxes that the formal sector pays. We also employ many people. Some major wholesalers might have five or six people working with them in the distribution chain. We also create more jobs in the formal sector, like in travel agencies.

The new foreign-exchange liberalisation isn't helping the Jamaican economy. It's very hard when a trader has to find 20,000 Jamaican dollars in order to buy 1,000 US dollars. Even with 3,000 US dollars you can't go to Panama as a wholesaler to shop; you need at least 5,000 or 10,000. So you've got to put up 100,000 Jamaican dollars up front. Despite the liberalised system, the local banks can't supply the local demand. You have to wait up to a month if you want 500 US dollars. People who get hold of foreign exchange now just keep it for themselves in their own accounts.

We believe in a free-market system, but not a system where you liberalise some parts but hold on to others. There's still a barricade against us. For example, Grace Kennedy have a tin of cooking oil at almost 1,000 dollars. We higglers found a way of bringing in that same four-gallon tin of cooking oil and when they were selling it for 600 dollars, we were selling it for 400 and something. Immediately, a protection barrier was installed at the airport, and when they saw they couldn't stop it from coming in, they went as far as to go the supermarkets which had already bought it and locked them up and took it away! Just to force people not to buy from us. If we can bring something into this country and sell it much cheaper to the consumer, then why should the government try to stop us? Is it liberalisation for one sector and not for another?

We are saying that the small entrepreneur must be encouraged. When the country was in crisis in the 1970s, when the government and the IMF policies were failing in the last part of the 1970s, when everybody was running away, it was these people who stayed behind. Whether sun, rain or storm, the higgler is always working. Even if the formal sector tries to take over our export business, they'll fail. Because the importers in places like the Cayman Islands believe in us small traders. When a flight is going there you don't find many formal businessmen on it. It's full of higglers, and each one is carrying five or ten boxes of agricultural produce into the Caymans. So there's a regular weekly supply.

We have to tackle the drug question. Some people are looking for a short cut, rather than trading in the normal way. Some of the goods coming in from Panama and Curacao have to be enforced. We're becoming a trans-shipment point between those territories and Miami. We have to stop our people getting involved with this, because it gives higglering a bad name. In Miami and New York there are a lot of people involved with drugs, some of them behind bars. As an organisation, we don't want to deal with these people. But we have to admit that some people in this trade do get caught up with drugs. They want a house in Beverly Hills or a new Nissan, but without working for it.

The debt is not going down, but going up. The same two governments have been playing with us for years. Between 1980 and 1989 the debt went up from 980 million dollars to five billion dollars. This is more money than the people of Jamaica have ever had since Christopher Columbus discovered the island! The money's been used to keep one government in power or to get another one in. Billions have been invested in projects that have never been finished. Now we're told that we, the traders and tax-payers, have to pay it back. It's not us as individuals who created the debt, but irresponsible governments who people still look up to.

Goods are on the shelves, but people just can't afford them. When a man has to pay J$10.20 for a loaf of bread, it's serious. When you look at a family of 10 or 15, you're talking about malnutrition and suffering. We are traders, but we have our brothers' and sisters' interests at heart. Because if they don't consume the goods we have, we'll get nowhere.

The teacher

Donaldson Bernard is Principal of the Port Antonio Secondary School in Port Antonio, Portland. It is a school for those children who fail the Common Entrance examination at the age of twelve, and specialises in vocational training. Portland is one of the poorer rural parishes in Jamaica, where services and infrastructure have traditionally lagged behind other areas.

In theory at least, education in Jamaica is available to all children from the age of six up to the age of twelve. At that point we find quite a lot of them stopping their education, although they should move either into the All Age Schools or into a Secondary School like this one. Those who have passed the Common Entrance go to the High School. Those who don't come to a Secondary School, and this is one of our problems here because the parents feel that the children have already failed and are less willing to devote the resources to their education.

In some areas you may find the level of achievement at the Secondary School comparable to that at the High School. But the big difference is that we specialise in vocational skills. Some of the brighter children are prepared for examinations such as the GCE and CXC, but that isn't our main focus. Our students are expected to sit the Secondary School Certificate, the exam that has been designed for the students in the new Secondary Schools.

From the outset of the economic crisis in Jamaica schools have received very little in the way of new equipment and we have been unable to maintain existing equipment. For example, here we do a lot of woodworking, metalworking and auto-mechanics, but not all of the lathes in those sections are functioning. New equipment is out of the question, not just expensive items such as that, but also basics. For years I've been asking the Ministry for desks for the school office, and we haven't got proper typewriters. When we have a lot of typing to do we have to borrow machines from the business education department.

Another area is building. It means that new buildings are not provided, even though we're running out of space here and need additional classrooms. There is also the problem of maintenance. The grant doesn't grow, but costs are rising and it becomes more and more impossible to maintain buildings and fittings. We have a serious problem here, because when this became a Junior Secondary School it had about 800 students. Now we have about 1,500 students – it was up to 2,400 at one time – and we still have the original toilet facilities. These are completely inadequate and repairing them is a constant problem. Before hurricane Gilbert struck, many of our roofs were leaking and sometimes we had to close the school during bad weather. The school has been refurbished since the hurricane and there has been some improvement.

We receive less money each year to provide class materials although the cost has gone up. In the old days the Ministry used to employ a per capita formula in allocating resources to schools. Now I don't know on what basis they decide how much each school should get. Last year we got about 55,000 dollars for some 1500 children, and that includes all stationery, repairs to any machinery in the different departments, anything the teachers might need. For example, the business education department needs about 20 new typewriters, but all we can do is keep repairing the old ones and some of them are beyond repair. We also need sewing machines, but the only one we have got was from a charitable organisation.

I was aiming here for a class size of about 35 to 40. In fact, there are some classes with fewer than 35 students. But there are other classes which have 40-odd, and last year we had a class of 49 students. This arises because we have been trying to stream the students, and what we found this year was that more than half the children who came in at Grade 7 needed remedial attention. So, although on paper one can work out an average class size of under 40, the fact is that the remedial groups have been larger than we wanted them to be. But at this level, even a class size of 40 is too big. Teachers face real discipline problems, especially with the lower achievers. These are the hardest ones to control. There is also the problem of different ability levels in large classes.

Now we have to insist that the parents make contributions. We can't force them to, but we put a lot of pressure on them to make the contributions because that is the only way that we manage to do anything at all. But the ability of parents to do this has been

Salaries have failed to keep pace with rising prices and many teachers are forced to take second jobs to make ends meet.

reduced over time. We're currently asking for 100 dollars per child per year. It's less than at other schools, but in this parish parents have not been accustomed to making that type of contribution. Though it may seem a small amount, we don't manage to collect it from many parents. We also operate a tuck shop, where we sell drinks and snacks. This is what we're using to try to buy typewriters. At the rate we're going, I hope that every two months we should be able to buy one typewriter. We have other fundraising efforts from time to time; sometimes we rent out the school buildings for meetings and other events, and we charge a fee.

Teachers' salaries have definitely fallen behind the cost of living. A trained teacher has a salary scale between 24,426 and 27,018 dollars per year, and a teacher with a diploma has a scale between 29,046 and 31,716. At the top scale, a teacher with a degree and training gets between 32,685 and 35,910. You don't find many teachers with degrees in the primary school sector, but there the salaries are the same. We've just accepted the government's offer for the forthcoming year, so principals and vice-principals will receive a 10 per cent salary increase, and other teachers will receive a 15 per cent increase.

Because of inflation and the rising cost of living, real salaries have been left behind. This affects the quality of new teachers and the morale of those already in the profession. It also affects the amount of time that the teacher spends with the students. When I was a junior teacher it was commonplace for a teacher to remain behind after school to give extra assistance to a child or to help with extra-curricular activities. Nowadays, especially in a shift school like this, the morning teacher finishes work and goes out to try to do something else. We had a teacher – he's no longer with us – who used to go and work at a supermarket, supervising sales in the wholesale department. There are others who teach part-time at another school. There are teachers who also do some higgling, who go to Miami and bring things over to sell. It means that the extra-curricular activity at this school is practically non-existent. Teachers are too busy trying to do something else to supplement their salary to give the children that sort of attention. We even have problems with absenteeism. I had one teacher who was regularly absent on Thursdays, and I found out that he was going every Thursday to Ocho Rios to do something connected with the cruise ships.

This is the worst aspect of the problem. After all the deprivation that children in this type of school suffer, coming from poor homes and suffering from low expectations on the part of their parents, they don't get the support which they need from their teacher. It's a shame.

Here, teachers were once considered middle-class – and still are – but the fact is that the teacher lives a lower-class sort of life despite education and aspirations. Most teachers cannot consider taking on a mortgage, even for housing specifically built as low-income accommodation. Some get round it by making joint applications and sharing housing. Apart from those who are able to supplement their salary in some way, teachers cannot afford to buy cars. I am a principal, but my car is now 19 years old and I can't seriously consider buying a new one.

Since the petrol crisis in 1974 things have been going from bad to worse. But in recent times there has been a noticeable decline in people's quality of life because of the sharp fall in the value of the Jamaican dollar. The situation has been deteriorating over time, but recently there has really been a discernible decline.

I don't think that teachers as a whole discuss the reasons for this enough. The main teachers' organisation, the JTA, doesn't deal with this as an issue on which teachers should take a stance. The other teachers' union, the NUDT, makes statements as to how the government should treat IMF conditionality and so on, but I don't think that teachers deal with this question enough, perhaps because it is seen as politics.

We need to restore a certain minimum quality of life to the teacher, because everything starts with the teacher. Even given inadequate materials, a good, dedicated teacher will achieve a lot. But right now, the whole profession is so demoralised that even given new buildings and equipment, not much can be done. We also need a better system of monitoring, and here again the whole economic situation has made things worse, since the Ministry of Education can't send out its education officers often enough. They do not have the resources with which to travel around and monitor activities within the schools. This is a vital part of the whole system.

Our children go on work experience, and they are placed in various work environments for two weeks to see what it is really like to work. They're not paid a salary but they get that experience. Sometimes they actually get jobs during that time and we have problems persuading them to remain at school. That's true, for instance, of those who do catering and are placed in the hotels. So we do have some kind of success with some of our students. Those who do catering are the best off, but others, such as woodworking students, go off and start their own little furniture-making business. Sometimes they come back to school to use the lathes and the teachers help them out. This is the kind of thing I would like to see us develop more. The children are going to have to create their own jobs.

We need to know exactly what needs there are on the job market and adjust what we do in school accordingly. I think that we have to develop the kinds of skills that the parish needs and make sure that our vocational training will help the children to find a job when they leave. This will also form part of the whole development process.

Nursery class, part of a multi-purpose centre at Port Antonio, supported by Oxfam.

Lenford Mattis trained in horticulture with Oxfam help, and now runs a successful tree-nursery. He demonstrates (left) a technique for grafting a high-yielding variety of mango on to a native stock. Farmers benefit from the improved quality of fruit they can produce.

4

Oxfam in Jamaica

Oxfam set up an office in Jamaica in 1985. Before that, although Oxfam supported some projects in the country, there was no permanent presence and the programme was administered from offices elsewhere in the region, with staff making periodic visits to keep in touch with project partners.

The emphasis before 1985 was on support to intermediate non-governmental organisations (NGOs) based in Kingston. Some of these NGOs sought to tackle urban poverty, while others targeted the poor in rural areas. Oxfam also supported legal aid needs through the Jamaica Council for Human Rights, and worked with people with disabilities through Deeds Industries Limited.

Since 1985, the programme has sharpened its focus, based on Oxfam's understanding of the causes of poverty in Jamaica and identification of the areas of most acute need. Economic and social policies of successive governments in response to IMF/World Bank prescriptions have resulted in a decline of government services to farmers in rural areas. Small farmers have problems in getting access to credit, and face fierce competition from imported food items; they also find difficulty in marketing their produce. Oxfam supports NGOs working in rural areas, such as the Social Action Centre and the Roman Catholic Human Development and Social Justice Commission, who help rural community-building projects and farmers' organisations and provide agricultural extension services.

Oxfam has also provided material inputs through farmers' organisations. The Hillside Farmers' Association is one such group, for which Oxfam provided piping for improved irrigation systems. Seeds and fertilisers have been provided for farmers in

Balaclava and St Elizabeth, and advice and assistance with food crops and fish-farming for other co-operatives.

Economic liberalisation policies have led to high interest rates and changes in legislation which make it possible for individual Credit Unions to set their own rates of interest. Farmers and other people running small businesses have very little access to cheap credit. Oxfam has made a contribution to establishing alternative credit facilities for small farmers in the hope that even the limited funds available will make a significant difference in enabling farmers to improve their situation.

It has been estimated that about one in three Jamaican households are headed by women; but women have a higher rate of unemployment than men, and the jobs available to women tend to be poorly paid and insecure. Oxfam has recognised the special needs of women and given grants to women's organisations, such as the Sistren Theatre Collective and the Association of Women's Organisations of Jamaica, which seek to empower women by building their self-esteem and awareness, and providing skills training and continuing education.

In 1988 Oxfam provided immediate disaster relief in the aftermath of Hurricane Gilbert, which caused widespread destruction. Oxfam also provided help with reconstruction, and trained community builders in hurricane-resistant building practices.

Although small projects can transform individual lives, their impact is of necessity limited. Oxfam is also involved in initiatives to encourage NGOs to undertake research to deepen their understanding of effective strategies to help poor people, and to foster networking and collaboration between NGOs to increase the effectiveness of their development programmes.

More recently, Oxfam has supported a project in which government and NGOs work together. Government-funded sanitation and immunisation programmes are combined with NGO projects to promote community participation, so that poor people in marginalised urban communities can play a part themselves in improving their health and living conditions.

Notes

Introduction

1 Levitt K P (1991) *The Origins and Consequences of Jamaica's Debt Crisis, 1970-1990*, Kingston, Jamaica; University of the West Indies.

2 Ibid., p.34

An overview of the Jamaican economy

1 Thomas C Y (1988) *The Poor and the Powerless: Economic Policy and Change in the Caribbean*, New York: Monthly Review Press.

2 Williams E (1970) *Columbus to Castro: The History of the Caribbean 1492-1968*, London: Andre Deutsch.

3 *Report of the West India Royal Commission*, appointed 1938. HMSO, CMD 6607, 6608, 1945.

4 Girvan N (1972) *Foreign Capital and Economic Underdevelopment in Jamaica*, Kingston, Jamaica: Institute of Social and Economic Research, University of the West Indies.

5 Beckford G and Witter M (1982) *Small Garden, Bitter Weed: Struggle and Change in Jamaica*, London: Zed Press.

6 Witter M and Kirton C (1990) *The Informal Economy in Jamaica: Some Empirical Exercises*, Working Paper 36, Kingston, Jamaica: Institute of Social and Economic Research, UWI.

7 Jefferson O (1972) *The Postwar Economic Development of Jamaica*, Kingston, Jamaica: ISER, UWI.

8 Thomas C Y 'The Economic Crisis and the Commonwealth Caribbean: Impact and Response', Paper presented at the Institute of Social and Economic Research, University of the West Indies and UNRISD Conference on Economic Crisis and Third World Countries: Impact and Response, Jamaica, 1989.

9 Kirton C 'Capital Flight and Foreign Debt: Notes on the Jamaican Experience', Paper presented to 13th Regional Monetary Studies Conference, Belize, 1987.

10 Statistical Institute of Jamaica (STATIN) and Planning Institute of Jamaica (PIOJ) (1989) *Survey of Living Conditions, July 1989, Jamaica*.

Further reading

James Ferguson, *Far From Paradise: An Introduction to Caribbean Development*. London, Latin America Bureau, 1990.

Kari Polanyi Levitt, *The Origins and Consequences of Jamaica's Debt Crisis, 1970-1990*. Kingston, University of the West Indies, 1991.

Neil MacDonald, *The Caribbean: Making Our Own Choices*. Oxford, Oxfam Publications, 1990.

Kathy McAfee, *Storm Signals: Structural Adjustment and Development Alternatives in the Caribbean*. London, Zed Books, 1991.

Social Action Centre, *Hooked on Debt*. Kingston, Social Action Centre for the Association of Development Agencies (ADA), 1990.

Clive Y. Thomas, *The Poor and the Powerless: Economic Policy and Change in the Caribbean*. London, Latin America Bureau, 1988.